A GLIMPSE OF THE RAINBOW

AN INSIGHT INTO THE LGBTQIA+ COMMUNITY

FRANCIS H. FERNANDES

Made with ♥ on the Notion Press Platform
www.notionpress.com

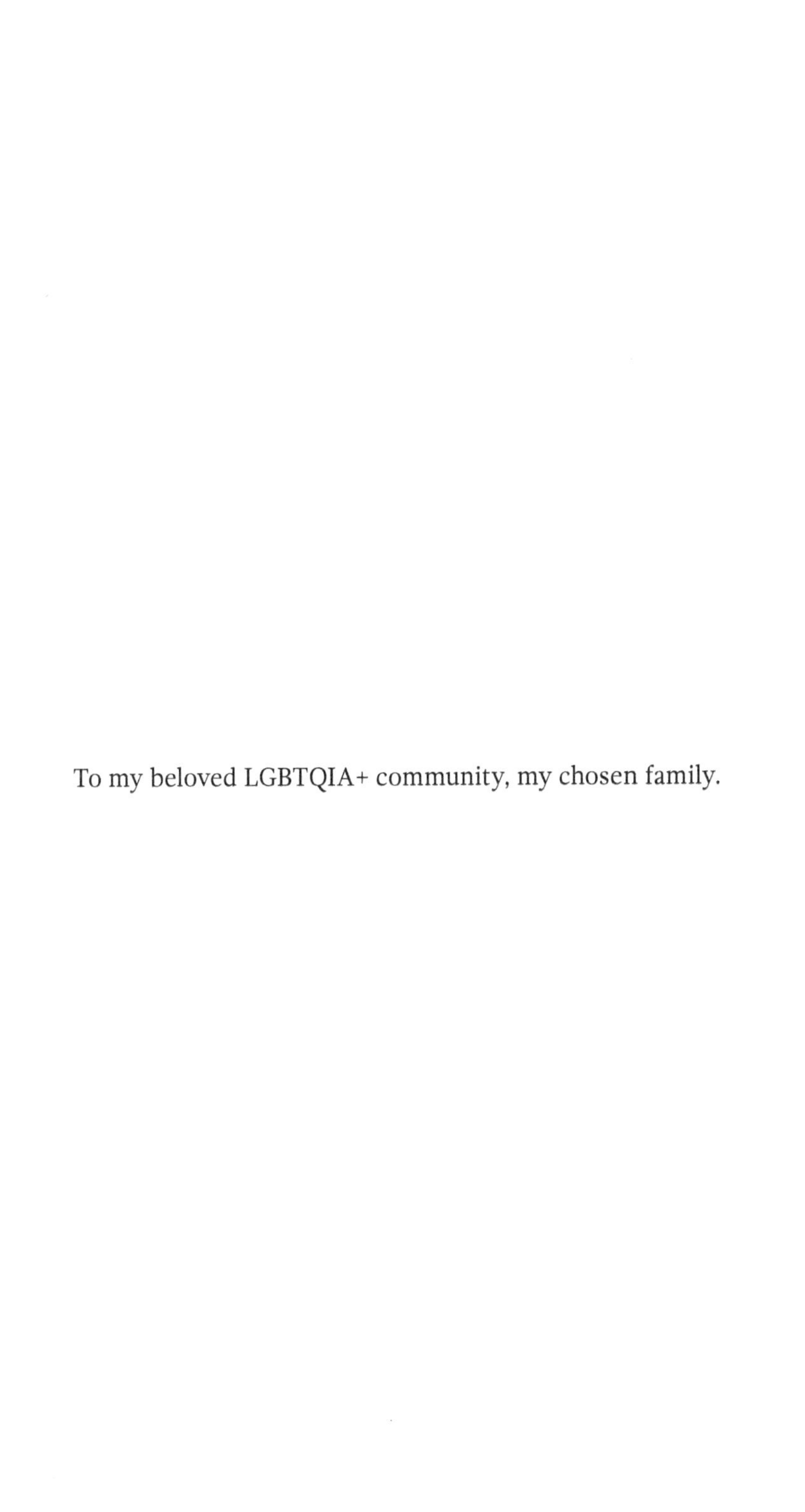

To my beloved LGBTQIA+ community, my chosen family.

Contents

Preface

*"Diversity is acceptable, divisiveness is not —
Francis H. Fernandes"*

A rainbow is synonymous with the phrase "unity in diversity." Each one of us represents a shade of color, and when we come together and uphold the values of humanity, love, compassion, mutual respect and individuality, we enable the formation of the beautiful band of colors we know as a rainbow. Our diversity does not mean that we deserve hatred because of our differences, but that embracing our differences increases the beauty of the world.

Despite centuries of struggle for inclusion and promoting diversity, we have not yet eliminated inequalities in society. One community that suffers the most from discrimination because of these inequalities is the LGBTQIA+ community. It is time that we dismantle the systems that continue to oppress this vibrant community by taking a glimpse of the rainbow.

Acknowledgements

Writing this book has been a worthwhile experience for me personally as well as one that has allowed me to educate the readers.

I want to express my gratitude to everyone who contributed to the development of this book, regardless of whether they were involved directly or indirectly. I would like to extend my sincere appreciation to everyone who filled out the survey I used for my study. I sincerely value the insights you provided.

Rishabh, Asher, Veda, Gautam, Yuuhi, Surya, Ryle, Uttaran, Roshan, Andy, Nihal, Daniel, Divya, Akshita, Nishica, Anthony, Noel, Sandeep, Abhishek, Smitin, Raj, Meghna, Nesara, Sushant, Parmesh, and Alok are just a few of the people who have encouraged me to write about my dearest community. I admire your dedication to advocating for our community while creating an inclusive society in your own unique ways

Disclaimer

This book includes references to adult sex, violence, sexual abuse, rape, suicide, murder, assault, castration, torture, and death. Readers are encouraged to use caution.

The author does not intend to hurt any religious, national, or cultural sentiments with any opinions mentioned in any of the chapters. The statements are explicitly his personal views on the treatment of the LGBTQIA+ community by various faiths, nations, or cultures.

CHAPTER ONE

MY PERSONAL QUEER JOURNEY

On August 24, 1994, I was born in the State of Kuwait as my parents' first child. They were very excited when I, a male child, entered their lives after 12 years of marriage. I was told that my relatives in India celebrated with fireworks when they heard the news. I was raised Roman Catholic and was constantly taught that Jesus Christ was my Lord and Savior, and I felt very attached to my religion. To almost everyone, I seemed to be a humble believer, but over time something changed that altered my religious identity.

Growing up, I was always attracted to some boys and men—those I knew personally as well as strangers who caught my attention when they passed me. However, I had no idea what that feeling was because every piece of media I consumed, every couple I saw, the religious beliefs I was raised with, and everything else around me forced me to believe that I should and could only be attracted to girls or women. As a result, I swept my feelings under the rug out of fear—of "God", my family, my school, the public, and all the people in my life. I thought I could play the role of a heterosexual man, as I was expected to do. I even tried asking a few girls out while I was in school and during my early college days, but although I could imagine a romantic relationship with some of them, I felt no sexual attraction. I remember admiring the bare-chested men on TV and having this unknown fire burning in my heart. It was so hard to comprehend what was going on in my mind, heart and body. Nonetheless, it felt heavenly. It was not until 2006 that I knew what it meant to be gay, but I had not yet accepted that I was. I lived in denial to the point where I wished I did not exist. I was suicidal for many years and even attempted to take my own life several times, but I kept reminding myself that it was not up to me to decide when my life would end. A few months before my final move to India, I assumed I might be bisexual. Even though this assumption relaxed my mind to a certain extent, my inability to develop a sexual attraction toward women kept me awake at night.

Kuwait was a great place to be born and bred, but it also had its drawbacks. Because of the diversity in the expatriate community, I was able to have a slightly larger perspective on the world as a young, closeted, and confused adolescent. I recognized and valued the diversity of origins, ethnicities, and faiths present around the globe. I came to understand that although we are all quite different from one another as human beings, it was valid. I knew that homosexual people faced religious opposition, but I was unaware that Kuwait's laws were anti-LGBTQIA+ at the time. I didn't realize the magnitude of homophobia in the legislation until I recently initiated a Google search and was shocked to see that it mostly pertained to male individuals alone. Since then, I've been at odds with myself for revering Kuwait as the go-to city to live in. I recurrently regret having been born in a country that takes pride in its bigotry to this very day.

I guess the famous quote "Everything happens for a reason" is truer than we make it out to be. I say this because I was very down when I knew that we had to move to India for good. I had spent almost 17 years of my life in Kuwait. I had made a handful of friends there and was just starting to live my life. But the move led to my eureka moment. I finally had a broadband connection that allowed me to access the internet with ease. I watched videos of gay men coming out on YouTube, listened to their encouraging advice, signed up for a gay dating website, met my first boyfriend, and was accepted into a WhatsApp group for gay and bisexual Indian men. All of these helped me get closer to my inner being and my queerness. The YouTube videos made me think about my feelings as a child—the fact that I was always attracted to boys and men. This confirmed and helped me accept that I was indeed gay. Now it was time to let the world in on my little secret, but just the thought of coming out scared the shit out of me because I was aware that I could possibly lose my family and friends forever. At the same time, I did not want to spend my life with someone I could not make happy, and could not ruin a woman's life by marrying her and dating men behind her back at the same time. I was not raised with the value of being inconsiderate of another person. So I decided to harness every bit of courage inside me and come out of the closet.

I had always been a very shy and introverted person. I could never really verbalize many of my thoughts and feelings. Saying the words "I am gay" out loud turned out to be far more intimidating than I had anticipated. So I opted for the rather comfortable alternative in text form. I typed my coming-out message on my laptop and reviewed the list of potential recipients, keeping in mind their possible reactions. My original plan was to send the message to my classmates in college, so I started with my best friend at the time, Siddhant. At first, he was shocked and could not digest it because I had previously mentioned that I had a "crush" on a female batchmate. But when I assured him that I was definitely gay, he comforted me with his acceptance. This was an encouraging and motivating experience that prompted me to come out to another classmate. He too responded with the same acceptance and support. This was when I realized that I needed to let my parents in on this part of my life before they found out about it from someone else. I was so hell-bent on doing it that I contemplated telling my family on my twenty-first birthday, right after I cut my birthday cake. Fortunately, Siddhant strongly advised against it and suggested that I wait to do it at a later time. He once again stopped me from making a hasty mistake and telling my family during my semester finals, so I decided to postpone it till my exams were over.

The evening after my last paper, I felt a pit in my stomach that made me nauseous. My heart was pounding so hard that it could jump out of my body. My silence at the dinner table and my sluggish eating gave my mother a hint that something was wrong. I sobbed and shook as I tried to push the food down my throat. After an hour had passed, I was finally done. I cleaned up and prepared to break the news to my parents and younger brother. I attempted to get the words out three times, but I could not. My mother then took me into another room and asked me what was wrong. After more crying and silence, I finally blurted it out. She seemed confused and could not comprehend what I had said. When I told her that I liked men and answered in the affirmative to her question about whether I wanted to marry a man, she was not very pleased. She claimed that it was only "in my head" and that I would be fine if I just "prayed to God". After all, for a pious mother, prayers were considered the only solution to any problem. However, it never worked for me. I had tried that for years before I accepted my gayness for myself. So I decided to keep telling my friends and keeping the rest of my family in suspense. Every single person I came out to after that was very supportive and accepting of who I am. Even those who disagreed with the idea of being gay said they were happy for me as long as I was pleased with who I am. That was a great relief. A huge weight had been lifted off my shoulders. I felt that I could finally live my life as an openly gay man. I also decided to send my message to my younger brother, and I was so happy to learn that he was cool about it. He mentioned that he "already knew" because I had shared many LGBTQIA+-related posts from various sources on social media in the past.

When I was about to graduate from college, I decided to make my truth public. I inserted my same coming-out message into a caption and posted it on Facebook and Instagram. That was the moment the reality of the world hit me. Among the many heartfelt responses I received from friends and even absolute strangers were some pretty hurtful ones. These hit me right in the heart. I knew that there were ignorant people in the world, but it was not their life to decide how to live it. It was not their place to tell me that I was doing something wrong. It was not their place to decide that I was not who I claimed to be. They were not in my body. They could not feel what I was feeling. So how could they just assume that my identity was invalid? How could they disregard the fact that I was also human? How could they not realize that I was allowed to be different from everyone else?

In 2017, I had the opportunity to participate in my first Pride parade in Goa. I was thrilled to be a part of it. It was my next step into a life of transparency. I could come out of my shell and be proud, and stand by who I was without fearing anyone or anything. Anything but being the victim of a violent hate crime. After all, I was a human being too. I lived in a city whose roots were deep in religion and traditions, and in a time when extremism was burgeoning in the minds of conservative folk. I had read social media posts reporting hate crimes against LGBTQIA+ individuals in other parts of India. Nonetheless, my first Pride experience was beyond great. It also marked the beginning of my journey to activism. It encouraged me to advocate for my community, further educate myself about it, and also sensitize the masses as best I could.

In addition to the historic Supreme Court ruling overturning Section 377, 2018 brought me the privilege of co-founding an NGO with two other young queer activists, Chris and Rishabh. At that time, my mother seemed to slowly learn to accept who I was. She still had a long way to go and many more instances of falling back on the anti-LGBTQIA+ mentality, but I could see a sign of hope. My father, on the other hand, was definitely aware of my identity, although I never mentioned it to him, but did not comment on it and has not done so to this day. But nothing would deter me from living my truest life. From organizing a Pride parade to meeting fashion designer late Wendell Rodricks, filmmaker Apurva Asrani, activists Harish Iyer, Ashok Row Kavi, Vivek Anand and Asha Vernekar, and many other notable figures in the field, I slowly grew out of my introversion. I felt more confident being myself than hiding. I had managed to take a few steps toward happiness. This was also the year I met and fell in love with a young man. I was hopeful that I would climb to the next stage of my life as an openly gay man—finding love. However, the relationship only lasted 3 weeks, but the hope that we would eventually get back together enticed me to hold on to our friendship.

With each day spent at NGO, I grew through 2019 to fulfill my childhood desire of giving back to others. Little did I know that it would be one of my worst years. The man I loved so dearly cut ties with me without any explanation. I was devastated. I tried to stay strong, but I felt suicidal all the time. The NGO and my friends helped me get through most days. They say that every cloud has a silver lining, and I should've anticipated that the following year would fundamentally change my life, especially for the better.

The year 2020, as we know it, was the year of the COVID-19 pandemic. It swept the world by surprise. However, I published my maiden book, Music To My Poetry, in the first month. The book was a compilation of poems I had written over two years, with some very personal ones. Yet it wasn't the part that altered my life. In February, I bought my first pair of high-heeled shoes—platform booties with a three-inch block heel. While in lockdown in the month of September, I took advantage of the opportunity and purchased something that I have wanted for a very long time. As I was browsing an e-commerce website, I came across a pair of champagne-colored five-and-a-half-inch-high peep-toe stiletto pumps and decided to buy them. I was overjoyed when they arrived and I tried them on for the first time. I was privileged to have the ability to embrace a dimension of myself that I had long been embarrassed about—my femininity. As male individuals, we are compelled to adhere to the strict cisheteronormativity that is imposed on us. Our acceptance of our femininity is viewed as an insult to boys and men. Dresses, skirts, blouses, crop tops, sarees, beauty care products, and high-heeled footwear if worn by men are considered to be weak and repulsive by society. Boys playing with dolls and even preferring the color pink is taboo in many families. I was fortunate enough to be born during an era when such deleterious beliefs were being challenged. I was joyful as I grinned at myself in the mirror while wearing my sparkling stilettos. That joy kept me going further. I experimented with crop tops made from my t-shirts, and I even draped myself in a Sholapuri chaddar to imitate a skirt and a gown. From these experiences, I accepted my androgynous gender expression and I also learned that it is indeed acceptable for our preferences to differ from those of others as human beings. This year also served as a year of body positivity. I had been insecure about my skinny frame since I was a child. I would become very conscious of the same when I wore clothes that were too big for me. Shorts that cut above my knees were my least favorite because they highlighted my bony legs. It was not until I was introduced to the notion of creative nudity that I began overcoming my body insecurities. I started flaunting my legs in my really short shorts, at least those considered too short for men. I finally felt at peace with my body.

In addition to embracing my body and androgyny, Raj's initiative, Indian Asexuals, which aimed to educate and empower the asexual population in India, was something I had the privilege of learning about. Via their well-run webinars and engaging Instagram page, I learned about the aro-ace spectrum and was also able to self-identify as a homoromantic demisexual person. My interactions with Indian Asexuals also expanded my awareness of the variety of possible ways that people might identify, apart from sole allosexuals. After discovering the seven spectrums of attraction, I progressed to have great regard for every single person in the world. I came to see that every human is just as deserving of respect as any other, regardless of the many labels we may or may not employ. I was undoubtedly in a frame of mind where I felt good about myself and, consequently, optimistic about a brighter future for all of mankind.

Does this imply that I only get affection and good vibes from social media? I regrettably do not. Flash forward to 2023, and I have received a barrage of criticism for uploading bare-bodied photos that celebrate my body and for embracing femininity via my androgyny. The issue is exacerbated by the fact that certain members of our community, particularly cisgender men, employ cyberbullying tactics like femme shaming and body shaming in reaction to my authentic profile pictures on online dating sites like Grindr and Tinder. It is the same conditioning we are exposed to as children, that matures into this repulsive idea of bullying other people solely because they don't fit one's ideals of gender and sexuality. Nonetheless, I no longer allow their judgment to break me. To defend myself against the hostility I encounter, I have built a fortress of self-love and continue to live by my own rules. I presently own sarees, long shrugs, oxidized silver necklaces, four pairs of stilettos (one with nearly seven-inch high heels), and a few nail polishes. #slay.

I try my best to live my gayest life ever to inspire and encourage other members of my community to embrace their individuality. It would not be possible to do so if I hadn't been inspired myself. I owe my confidence and carefree spirit to the many individuals who taught me that since we only have one life to live, we ought to make the most of every day—my friends Rishabh, Asher, Veda, Ryle (Artrysis) and Yuuhi, celebrities, drag artists and activists Billy Porter, Elle Deran, Sam Smith, Lil Nas X, Lilly Singh, Alok Vaid Menon, Harish Iyer, Grace Banu, Suresh Ramdas, Matt Bernstein, Schuyler Bailar, Yash Sharma, Meghna Mehra, Alex (Maya The Drag Queen), Sushant (Rani Ko-HE-nur), Durga Gawde, Gautam (Mysticurl Flame), and many more such individuals. They have all been truly amazing.

Alright, enough about me. Let's have a look at some of the obstacles that our community has faced and continues to encounter.

CHAPTER TWO

A History Of Oppression And Erasure

The LGBTQIA+ community has been persecuted for centuries if not millennia. It's time for us to look at some of the LGBTQIA+ injustices that have been perpetrated in the past. The fact that some of these events occurred repeatedly demonstrates the validity of the adage "history repeats itself," which is interesting to observe.

Ancient Assyria adopted the practice of castrating gay servants and slaves in **2100 BCE**.

According to *The Code of Assura* from either the Old Assyrian Empire or the Middle Assyrian Empire, between **c. 1500 BCE – c. 1101 BCE**, "when a man is prosecuted and found guilty of having intercourse with a neighbor, he is to be regarded as polluted and turned into a eunuch." It was assumed that "neighbor" in this context referred to a fellow soldier, who was often a male individual.

In the *Torah* (Book of Leviticus), the Jewish prophet Moses forbade homosexuality and cross-dressing in **1200**

BCE, sentencing the former with the death penalty for both men an women.

Between **c. 1000 BCE – c. 500 BCE**, Section V (27) of *Fargard 8. Funerals and purification, unlawful sex* from the Vendidad, Avesta stated, "O Maker of the material world, thou Holy One! If a man voluntarily commits the unnatural sin, what is the penalty for it? What is the atonement for it? What is the cleansing from it? Ahura Mazda answered: 'For that deed there is nothing that can pay, nothing that can atone, nothing that can cleanse from it; it is a trespass for which there is no atonement, for ever and ever.'" This is an ancient book that forbade males from having sexual relations with one another. "Unnatural sin" in this passage implied sodomy. It considered a fairly normal deed an unforgivable crime. Even while Section V (26) of the same text purports to forbid forced manifestations of the "unnatural sin", the penalty specified shows that it was not considered one that deserved no atonement. The phrase "the guilty may be executed by anybody, without an order from the Dastur, and by this execution, an ordinary capital offense may be redeemed" appeared as a note to Section V (32) of the same document. This promoted the patriarchal attitude of control over others by giving anybody who believed that homosexuality was evil the ability to use violence.

In **c. 700 BCE**, castrating homosexual slaves and household servants was a discipline that was brought to Persia from areas that the Neo-Assyrian Empire and the Median Empire had conquered. This highlights the persecution of those who were viewed as belonging to disadvantaged class levels and serves as an example of violence against homosexual individuals. It represents the persecution of the LGBTQIA+ community on an intersectional basis.

The *Book of Leviticus* was written between **c. 538 – 330 BCE**, and according to Leviticus 18:22 and Leviticus 20:13 it was forbidden to have sex with a man as with a woman, and both men would have committed an abomination and would have to be put to death since their blood was on them. With this, we have yet another ancient literature that forbade males from having intimate relations, thus upholding patriarchy and awarding the death penalty to mere acts of love. Ironically, loving one's neighbor was regarded as the most important commandment in the collection of texts that contains this very Book of Leviticus: the Bible.

For Persian Jews living in the Achaemenid Empire in **c. 486 BCE**, King Darius I adopted the *Holiness Code of Leviticus*, which established the first-ever state-sanctioned execution of males involved in same-sex partnerships.

In **350 BCE**, Plato criticized homosexuality in his book *Laws*, calling it lustful, bad for society, and potentially creating irresponsible citizens. He continued to write that homosexuality was also seen as a threat to the species since it did not advance the species, and his ignorant ideology is evidence of the lack of rational thinking in the human race. Since people with heterosexual interests are thought to outnumber those with same-sex inclinations, it would be impossible to stop our species from procreating.

Phillip II of Macedon and his son Alexander the Great destroyed the Sacred Band of Thebes, a gay army of more than 300 troops, in **338 BCE**.

In **300 BCE**, India's *Manusmriti (Manu Samhita)* did not explicitly ban homosexual activity but classified it as a minor sin for regular, twice-born males and for young, unmarried girls.

In **227 BCE, 226 BCE, 216 BCE, or 149 BCE,** the *Lex Scantinia* which was rarely mentioned or put into effect during the Roman Republic imposed punishments on those who committed a sex crime (stuprum) against a freeborn child. It may also have been applied to prosecute male citizens who voluntarily played a passive role in homosexual relationships. It is unclear if a fine or the death sentence was imposed.

Under Augustus's leadership in **27 BCE,** the Roman Empire was established. Roman citizens were subject to citizenship loss if they were discovered engaging in passive sexual behavior with another male and gay prostitution was taxed. Interestingly, many emperors who engaged in homosexual activity graced the throne of the Roman Empire throughout history while also enforcing laws that prohibited such acts.

Severus Alexander, an emperor in ancient Rome, banished gays who were involved in public life. Christius claims that Alexander toughened the laws against homosexuality across the Roman Empire somewhere between **222 – 235 CE.** Alexander reportedly considered outlawing male prostitutes, according to Historia Augusta.

Between **244 – 249 CE,** Marcus Julius Philippus, a Roman emperor, either tried to abolish male prostitution or successfully did so throughout the Roman Empire.

In **314 CE,** The Council of Ancyra which represented the Eastern European Church, prohibited unmarried males under the age of 20 who were found engaging in homosexual behavior from receiving the sacraments for 15 years and prohibited married men over the age of 50 from receiving the sacraments for life.

According to the book *The Life of Constantine,* the effeminate gay pagan priests who frequented the temple at

Aphaca in Phoenicia on the isolated peak of Mount Libanus between **306 – 337 CE** were ordered to demolish it by Roman emperor Constantine I. Moreover, it says that a decree enacted by Constantine mandated the execution of effeminate gay pagan priests in Egypt. This is only one of several probable recordings of what would be referred to be femme shaming in the present day and age. It is an indication that colonialism had a significant impact on the historical erasure and persecution of LGBTQIA+ persons.

The *Theodosian Code 9.7.3* issued by Constantius II and Constans I in **342 CE** states, "When a man marries in the manner of a woman, a woman about to renounce men, what does he wish, when sex has lost all its significance; when the crime is one which it is not profitable to know; when Venus is changed to another form; when love is sought and not found? We order the statutes to arise, the laws to be armed with an avenging sword, that those infamous persons who are now, or who hereafter may be, guilty may be subjected to exquisite punishment."

The Roman Empire made having intercourse with another man a crime in **370 CE**, and the punishment was death by burning.

Under Christian authority, Rome passed its first anti-homosexual statute in **389 CE**, denying homosexuals the ability to create or receive the benefits of wills.

The *Collatio Mosaic and Roman Laws* issued by Roman emperors Valentinian II, Theodosius I and Arcadius in **390 CE** state, "We cannot tolerate the city of Rome, mother of all virtues, being stained any longer by the contamination of male effeminacy, nor can we allow that agrarian strength, which comes down from the founders, to be softly broken by the people, thus heaping shame on the centuries of our founders and the princes, Orientius, dearly and beloved and favored. Your laudable experience will therefore punish among revenging flames, in the presence of the people, as required by the grossness of the crime, all those who have given themselves up to the infamy of condemning their manly body, transformed into a feminine one, to bear practices reserved for the other sex, which have nothing different from women, carried forth – we are ashamed to say – from male brothels, so that all may know that the house of the manly soul must be sacrosanct to all, and that he who basely abandons his own sex cannot aspire to that of another without undergoing the supreme punishment." The *Theodosian Code 9.7.6* issued by Roman emperors Valentinian II, Theodosius I and Arcadius during the same period states, "All persons who have the shameful custom of condemning a man's body, acting the part of a woman's to the sufferance of alien sex (for they appear not to be different from women), shall expiate a crime of this kind in avenging flames in the sight of the people." These appear to be two of the earliest examples of transgender identities being suppressed in history. The expression "abandons his own sex" emphasizes that one should preserve the sex assigned to them when they were born. Self-identity and bodily autonomy are denied.

For same-sex couples in **506 CE**, the *Visigothic Code* of Alaric II mandated burning at the stake. Additional penalties included castration, whipping, public ostracism, and head shaving.

According to Institutes IV. xviii.4 of the *Body of Civil Law* in the Byzantine Empire in **533 CE**, the Lex Julia de adulteris, which "...punishes with death, not only those who violate the marriages of others, but also those who dare to commit acts of vile lust with men," was one of the statutes that were used in public prosecutions in criminal cases.

Arianism was replaced by Catholicism in the Visigothic kingdom of Spain in **589 CE**. As a result of this conversion, the legislation was changed to reflect those of Catholic nations. Provisions for the persecution of Jews and homosexuals were included in these modifications. This appears to be a quintessential example of intersectional mistreatment of LGBTQIA+ individuals on the basis of faith. It draws attention to how the abuse of authority and coerced religious conversions result in the persecution of populations that are regarded as minorities. It isn't surprising that this persecution persists in the current era given the relatively strong pull that religion seems to have by blocking individuals from reasoning for themselves.

The seventh century saw the creation of Shari'a Law in **632 CE**, which spread progressively throughout the Islamic world. In addition to flagellation, homosexuality was punishable by death by stoning, burning, collapsing a rock wall upon, or being thrown off a great height. I must point out that the mere mention of homosexuality in "religious law" across religions contributes to the evidence that the LGBTQIA+ community has always existed.

The *Visigothic Code* was created in Spain in **642 CE** and spread progressively throughout Christian Europe. It mandated castration or burning to death for anybody found guilty of "sodomy."

Castration was used as punishment for sodomy in the Visigothic Kingdom in **654 CE**. This was the first secular law in Europe to make sodomy a crime.

In **693 CE**, Egica of Hispania and Septimania, a Visigothic monarch in Iberia, urged that a Church council address the prevalence of homosexuality in the Kingdom. In response, the Sixteenth Council of Toledo drafted a resolution that Egica later ratified, which stipulated that homosexual actions should be punished by castration, exclusion from Communion, hair-shaving, one hundred lashes, and exile.

Muslim traders from the ninth century brought the practice of castrating gay slaves and household staff to northern China in **700 CE**.

After fifteen years on the throne, the Korean Emperor Hyegong was executed in **780 CE** because his followers could no longer tolerate his effeminate demeanor.

Castrating homosexual house workers and slaves became common practice in northern India around the year **1000** courtesy of Muslims who arrived there in the eleventh century.

In **1007**, the Decretum of Burchard of Worms argued that homosexual behavior should carry the same punishment as other sexual offenses like adultery, which was generally fasting.

In **1051**, in his work *Liber Gomorrhianus*, Peter Damian makes an argument for harsher penalties for clerics who disobey their obligation to combat "vices of nature." The phrase "homosexuality is against the order of nature" has been thrown around frequently. Yet if that were true, our community wouldn't have existed in the first place, which makes it absurd. Moreover, many species wouldn't share similarities with our community. However, over five hundred species across the globe exhibit characteristics that overlap with LGBTQIA+ identities.

In **1102**, the Council of London took action to make sure the English people understood that the practice of homosexuality was unlawful.

To remedy the vices inside the Kingdom, Baldwin II of the Kingdom of Jerusalem called the Council of Nablus in **1120** which ordered the burning of anybody who regularly engages in sodomy.

In **1140**, in his book *Concordia discordantium canonum*, the Italian monk Gratian makes the case that because sodomy entails the member being used against nature, it is the greatest of all sexual crimes. I think it's bizarre that there were and still are many who believe that engaging in consensual sexual activity is a "bigger sexual crime" than indulging in forced sexual activities like rape. It ought to be highlighted that most of these opinions and remarks come from cisgender male individuals, reinforcing the patriarchal system.

A resolution for the excommunication of sodomites was published in **1179** by the Third Lateran Council in Rome.

Beginning in France in **1184**, the Roman Catholic Inquisitions used torture to coerce confessions and executed homosexuals. For more than seven centuries, the Inquisitions were in place all across the world.

The Inquisition is launched in the Italian City-States by Pope Gregory IX in **1232**. For first-time and second-time sodomites, some cities demanded exile or amputation as penalties, and burning for third-time or recurrent offenders.

First-time sodomites were stripped of their testicles in the Kingdom of France in **1260**, followed by second-time offenders who were stripped of their member, and third-time offenders who were burnt. Women who were discovered engaging in same-sex activities risked being tortured or killed.

According to Thomas Aquinas in **1265**, the second worst lustful sin after bestiality was sodomy.

According to the *Coutumes de Beauvais* decree in **1283**, guilty sodomites would have their possessions seized in addition to being burnt. The families of those found guilty of sodomy would have suffered far more than just the loss of a loved one had their possessions been taken away. The general public would have been filled with dread as a result, and their successors would have carried that fear. It not only fosters a toxic atmosphere within the family, but it also makes it possible for other families to imitate the same toxicity.

Between **1308–1314**, charges of heresy, idolatry, and sodomy were used by Philip IV of France to order the arrest of all Templars, although these accusations were only a ruse to capture the order's wealth. On March 18, 1314, Notre Dame sentenced order leaders to death and had them burnt at the stake. The fact that the law was exploited to deprive individuals of their wealth is not unusual and indicates that power was abused. This illustrates that such anti-LGBTQIA+ policies have been employed in the past and are presently being replicated to persecute those who identify as LGBTQIA+ while enriching the affluent.

After refusing to cease his "unnatural" relationship with Hugh Despenser, the earl of Winchester's son, Edward II of England was horrifyingly executed in **1327**.

Under Firuz Shah Tughlaq of the Delhi Sultanate's Islamic authority in **1351**, male castration and slavery reached their heights in India.

Two persons who were put to death in the **1370s** in Antwerp were John van Aersdone and Willem Case. They were accused of engaging in same-sex relationships, which was forbidden and fiercely despised in medieval Europe. Due to the fact that records of Aersdone and Case have survived, they stand out. Giovanni Braganza and Nicoleto Marmagna of Venice were another 14th-century couple whose names are still remembered today. The statement that the records of the aforementioned couples "survived" suggests that those of other LGBTQIA+ persons were obliterated. This demonstrates that attempts to erase our existence have been made throughout history, some of which have been successful.

Transvestite prostitute John Rykener, also known as Johannes Richer and Eleanor, worked mostly in London (near Cheapside) but was also active in Oxford. In **1395**, he was detained and questioned for transvestism.

Three days of anti-homosexuality and anti-lust sermons by Bernardino of Siena in Florence, Italy, culminated with the burning of cosmetics, wigs, and other adornment-related items on a bonfire in **1424**. These lectures, combined with actions taken at the time by other clergy, reinforced attitudes toward homosexuality and encouraged the government to step up its persecution efforts. He also advocated for sodomites to be ostracized from society.

Nezahualcoyotl, a Tlatoani from Texcoco, passed rules in **1431** that made homosexuality a crime that would result in execution by hanging.

In **1432**, the "Night Officials," the first group created exclusively to pursue sodomy, were founded in Florence. Over the following 70 years, they detained roughly 10,000 men and boys and were successful in convicting about 2,000 of them, with the majority of them paying penalties.

In **1451**, Pope Nicholas V gives the Catholic Inquisition permission to prosecute sodomite males.

Between **1471 – 1493**, under Sapa Inca Topa Inca Yupanqui or Tpac Inca Yupanqui's time as emperor, he allegedly punished homosexuals, according to Garcilaso de la Vega's *Real Reviews of the Incas*. General Auqui Tatu of Yupanqui threatened to burn down entire villages if anybody indulged in sodomy and executed in the public square everyone for whom there was even a hint of sodomy in Acari valley. Yupanqui in Chincha destroyed their homes and any trees they had planted by burning them alive in great numbers.

In **1483**, sodomites were castrated, burnt, and stoned during the early stages of the Spanish Inquisition. Indictments for sodomy were brought against more than 1,600 persons between 1540 and 1700.

In **1494**, Girolamo Savonarola admonished Florence's populace for their "horrible sins" (mostly gambling and homosexuality) and urged them to abandon their young, beardless lovers.

The sodomy laws of Spain, which had previously only been enforced in urban areas, were toughened in **1497** by the King of Aragon Ferdinand and Queen of Castile and León Isabella. The degree of the offense equivalent to treason or heresy was raised, the standard of proof was lowered, and the use of torture to elicit confessions was authorized. Also taken into custody was the defendant's property.

The *Fatawa-e-Alamgiri*, which mandated a variety of forms of penalties for homosexuality, up to stoning to death for a Muslim, was created under the Mughal Empire in the **1500s** by combining many pre-existing Delhi Sultanate regulations. Around this same period, male gay intercourse was made illegal across Portuguese India by the Goa Inquisition.

Sandro Botticelli, an Italian artist, was accused of sodomy in a lawsuit in **1502**.

It is said that in **1513**, Vasco Nez de Balboa, a conquistador in present-day Panama, fed forty gay Natives to his dogs.

In **1523**, the first of several sodomy accusations were levied against Florentine artist Benvenuto Cellini.

The Holy Roman Empire established the death penalty for sodomy in **1532**.

The *Buggery Act 1533*, enacted by King Henry VIII in **1533**, made anal intercourse a capital offense across England.

Thirty homosexuals were burnt at the stake in Portugal between **1536 – 1821** as a result of the Portuguese Inquisition.

The *Laws in Wales Act 1542*, which extended the buggery law into Wales, received royal assent from Henry VIII in **1543**.

More than 100 homosexuals were executed by burning in Zaragoza, Spain, between **1570 – 1630** as a result of the Spanish Inquisition (1478-1834).

Castration of young male singers, known as castrati, was approved by Rome in **1599**.

In **1610**, male sodomy was made a crime and subject to the death penalty by a military order issued by the Colony of Virginia. Later that year, martial law was lifted following a change of power in the Virginia Colony, ending this edict.

Sodomy was made a crime in Brandenburg-Prussia in **1620** and was subject to the death penalty.

In **1624**, Virginia Colony resident Richard Cornish was prosecuted for sodomy and executed by hanging.

One of the earliest documented sodomites to be put to death in colonial America (Dutch-ruled New Amsterdam, now New York City) was Jan Creoli in **1646**. His body was "burned to ashes" after being garroted, or strangled to death with a rope.

Sarah White Norman was accused of engaging in "lewd behavior with each other upon a bed" with Mary Vincent Hammon in Plymouth, Massachusetts in March **1648**, marking the first documented prosecution for lesbian conduct in North America. Being a minor, Hammon was not prosecuted. In a separate incident, a gay military drummer serving at the French garrison at Ville-Marie, New France, was found guilty in Canada's first-ever criminal trial for the crime of homosexuality and given the death penalty by the local Sulpician priests. The drummer's life was saved thanks to a Jesuit intervention in Quebec City, but only if he agreed to serve as New France's first permanent executioner.

A statute banning sodomy that included a penalty for lesbian liaison was passed by the Connecticut Colony in **1655**.

Several hundred homosexuals were publicly executed at San Lazaro, Mexico, between **1656 – 1663** as part of Spain's well-publicized campaign to rid that nation of sodomy.

After being found guilty of sodomy with a servant in New Amsterdam in **1660**, Jan Quisthout van der Linde was bound in a sack, tossed into a river, and drowned.

In **1661** male-to-male sodomy was once more made illegal when the Colony of Virginia adopted the English common law.

In the Kingdom of Denmark in **1683**, "relations against nature" were declared a felony that carried the death sentence going forward.

One of the final public homosexual burnings in France took place in **1702** after a well publicized male prostitution scandal in Paris.

German authorities executed Catharina Margaretha Linck for female sodomy in **1721**.

In **1726** police in London conducted a raid on Mother Clap's molly house, which culminated in the execution of three men.

In Holland, 75 homosexuals were executed by being garroted in the City Hall cellars between **1730 – 1732** as part of a brutal drive to rid the nation of sodomy "from top to bottom."

The first law in Chinese history outlawing consensual nonprofit gay intercourse was issued in **1740** by the Kiangxi Emperor of the Qing Dynasty.

After marrying Anne Kristine Mortensdotter in a Lutheran church, Jens Andersson of Norway, who was assigned female at birth but identified as a man, was arrested in **1781** and placed on trial. "Hand troer at kunde henhre til begge Deele" ("He believes he belongs to both") was the response when questioned about his gender. This could represent one of the first accounts of someone who, in terms of the verbiage used today, might identify under the non-binary spectrum.

The death penalty for sodomy in New York State was abolished in **1796** in favor of a maximum fourteen-year prison sentence.

New York made sodomy punishable by a mandatory life sentence in prison starting in **1801**.

In **1803**, the Batavian Commonwealth and continental Europe witnessed the last recorded state-sanctioned execution of a man for same-sex sodomy.

The United States criminal code introduced the expression "crime against nature" for the first time in **1814**.

Same-sex sexual activity was once again illegal in Prussian-annexed territory in **1815** when the Duchy of Warsaw was annexed by both the Russian Empire and the Kingdom of Prussia.

After seducing a male soldier at Saint-Denis, the Marquis de Custine was assaulted and left for dead in **1824**. He was forced out of the closet by the controversy, but then bounced back and spent the rest of his life with his partner Edward St. Barbe as an open "sodomite."

Under *Article 995* of the penal code, the Russian Empire made muzhelozhstvo, which authorities interpreted to indicate anal intercourse between men, a crime in **1832**. Men who were found to be guilty had their legal rights revoked and were sentenced to four to five years in Siberia.

In Congress Poland, the Russian portion of Poland that was acquired following the Partitions of Poland when it became a part of the Russian Empire, homosexuality was made illegal in **1835** for the first time in history. In an isolated incident, James Pratt and John Smith were hung at Newgate Prison in London after being caught together in a private dwelling, being the last known execution for homosexuality in Great Britain.

In Great Britain, the punishment for sodomy was changed from death by hanging to life in jail after a revision to the criminal code in **1860**. The new code was implemented in all of the then-British colonies across the world, including India, Malaysia, Hong Kong, Canada, Australia, the Caribbean, etc., and it had a significant long-term impact there.

In **1861**, the death penalty for "buggery" was repealed in England after the *Offences Against The Person Act 1861* (which had not been used since 1836) was revised. The penalty was upgraded to imprisonment ranging from ten years to life. In the same year, British India's colonial administration enacted *Section 377*, making all gay relations illegal across the country.

The *Reich Criminal Code's Paragraph 175* made homosexuality a crime throughout the German Empire in **1871**. In early editions, the provision also rendered bestiality and homosexual activities between men illegal.

In 1935, the Nazis broadened the legislation; during the subsequent prosecutions, thousands perished in Nazi concentration camps. In the same year, the Brits classified the hijra people as a "criminal tribe."

In **1885**, the United Kingdom's Queen Victoria granted her royal assent to the *Criminal Law Amendment Act 1885*, whose Labouchere Amendment (Clause 11) prohibited oral sex between males but not women. According to a common myth, Victoria suppressed references to lesbianism from the Act because she refused to accept that women "did such things"; nevertheless, they had never been mentioned in the Act in the first place. Anal intercourse between males, often known as buggery, was already forbidden. Clause 11 states, "Any male person who, in public or private, commits, or is a party to the commission of, or procures or attempts to procure the commission by any male person of, any act of gross indecency with another male person, shall be guilty of a misdemeanor, and being convicted thereof shall be liable at the discretion of the court to be imprisoned for any term not exceeding two years, with or without hard labor."

In **1886**, the practice of homosexuality was once again prohibited in Portugal.

Following his trial, Oscar Wilde was tried and convicted of "gross indecency" in **1895** and awarded a two-year-long prison sentence with hard labor under the terms of the *Criminal Law Amendment Act 1885*.

The Ariston Hotel Baths became the target of the first recorded American police raid on a gay bathhouse on February 21 in **1903**, in New York City. Thirty-four men were arrested, twelve were charged with sodomy, and seven were awarded prison sentences that ranged from four to twenty years.

In an effort to repeal *Paragraph 175* in **1907**, the active head of the Gemeinschaft der Eigenen, Adolf Brand, wrote a paper "outing" the German imperial chancellor, Prince Bernhard von Bülow. The Prince cleared his name by suing Brand for libel; Brand was awarded an 18-month prison sentence. German immigrant Reverend Carl Schlegel was declared guilty of "homosexualism, Sodomy, or Uranism" in the same year after being tried by the city Presbytery. Schlegel is credited as supporting "the same laws" for "homosexuals, heterosexuals, bisexuals, and asexuals."

In **1924**, Henry Gerber's Society for Human Rights in Chicago, the country's first gay rights group, dissolved under police pressure after the organization operated for a few months.

In **1926**, Eve's Hangout, a popular lesbian café in Greenwich Village, was shut down during a police raid.

In **1929**, the repeal of *Paragraph 175* was approved by a Reichstag Committee on October 16; however, it was not taken into effect due to the emergence of the Nazis.

In **1933**, the German Workers' Party's National Socialist Party banned homosexual groups. Homosexuals were imprisoned in concentration camps, and the Nazis demolished the Institute for Sexual Research, which was founded by Magnus Hirschfeld, and also burned down its library.

Muzhelozhstvo, or "man sleeping with man," as it is known specifically in Russian, was once more a crime in the USSR in **1934** and carried a maximum sentence of five years in prison, with additional time added for coercion or the involvement of minors.

The German invasion in **1940** prompted the Netherlands to disband the Nederlandsch Wetenschappelijk Humanitair Komitee (Netherlands

Scientific Humanitarian Committee), and the majority of its archives were voluntarily destroyed; the remainder were confiscated by Nazi soldiers.

In **1945**, after the Holocaust, it was projected that between 3,000 and 9,000 homosexual people were killed in Nazi concentration and death camps, while an estimated 2,000 to 6,000 homosexual survivors were compelled to serve the entirety of their prison sentences under Paragraph 175 of the *German Criminal Code*.

When the "lavender scare" started in **1950**, 190 individuals throughout the United States were dismissed from government employment because of their sexual orientation.

Dale Jennings was arrested in Los Angeles in the spring of **1952** upon allegations of soliciting a police officer at a bathroom in Westlake Park, now MacArthur Park. The Mattachine Society received extensive coverage in the press as a result of his trial, and membership skyrocketed after Jennings contested the charges and a hung jury.

In **1953**, Senator McCarthy referred to the "Lavender Scare," which occurred alongside the Red Scare during World War II and the immediate post-war period and exposed communists and alleged homosexuals. Widespread support was given to McCarthy's strategies, and later that year President Eisenhower issued an executive order barring homosexuals from working for the federal government. Individuals were terminated because of their actual or suspected sexual orientation.

Alan Turing, a mathematical and computer prodigy, committed suicide by cyanide poisoning in **1954**, 18 months after being given the option of two years in prison or a year of libido-reducing hormone therapy as a penalty for homosexual behavior. In the same year, Lord Montagu,

Michael Pitt-Rivers, and Peter Wildeblood were among a slew of well-known persons who were convicted of homosexual offenses when British authorities carried out a purge of homosexuals in Society akin to that of Joseph McCarthy.

The Johns Committee, also known as the Florida Legislature Investigative Committee, was created in **1956**. It examined gays as a national security concern while failing to uncover communist connections to civil rights organizations.

Scholars have claimed that *Executive Order 10450* had been in effect prohibiting transgender people from serving in the US military since at least **1960**.

In **1961**, according to the Vatican, nobody was supposed to be allowed to take religious vows or be ordained inside the Roman Catholic Church if they were "affected by the perverse inclination" toward homosexuality.

In **1965**, engaging in private, consensual sexual relations with men led to the arrest of Everett George Klippert, the last homosexual to be imprisoned in Canada. He received a "preventive detention" sentence for an indefinite period as a dangerous sexual offender after being assessed to be "incurably homosexual". Many Canadians believed this to be extremely homophobic, and sympathetic articles in *Maclean's* and *The Toronto Star* resulted in increased calls for legislative reform in Canada, which was eventually passed in 1969.

Twelve plainclothes police officers raided the Black Cat Tavern in Los Angeles' Silver Lake neighborhood on New Year's Day in **1967**, assaulting and arresting staff members and patrons. Following the raid, P.R.I.D.E (Personal Rights in Defense and Education) organized a series of protests that commenced on January 5.

The Stonewall riots, also known as the Stonewall uprising, Stonewall rebellion, or simply Stonewall, were a series of unannounced demonstrations by members of the gay community in response to a police raid that began in the early morning hours of June **28**, **1969**, at the Stonewall Inn in the Greenwich Village neighborhood of Lower Manhattan in New York City. As the police began behaving violently, Stonewall patrons, those at other lesbian and gay pubs in the Village, and locals on the streets retaliated. The riots are largely regarded as the pivotal event that changed the gay liberation movement and the twentieth-century American battle for LGBT rights.

On January 5, **1974**, authorities in Toronto arrested The Brunswick Four. The lesbian and gay community in Toronto was galvanized by this act of prejudice.

In the interest of broadening his anti-homosexual rights movement across the United States, Robert Grant founded the Christian Voice in **1976**.

In **1977**, a Human Rights Ordinance was passed in Dade County, Florida; it was overturned the same year as a result of a strident anti-homosexual rights campaign led by Anita Bryant.

Former Supervisor Dan White assassinated San Francisco Supervisor Harvey Milk and Mayor George Moscone in **1978**.

In **1981**, the Moral Majority began its campaign against homosexuality.

By **1982**, in addition to GRID5 (gay-related immune deficiency), "gay cancer," "community-acquired immune dysfunction," and "gay compromise syndrome," the illness that would become known as AIDS had many other names.

Reverend Jerry Falwell referred to AIDS as a "homosexual plague" in **1983**.

The Bowers v. Hardwick case was heard by the U.S. Supreme Court on June 30, **1986**. The court upheld a Georgia law that forbade oral or anal sex, ruling that homosexual relationships were not covered by the constitutional right to privacy. However, the court did not rule on whether the law could be applied to heterosexuals.

Until it was overturned in 2003, the anti-gay *Section 28* statute was implemented in England and Wales, and nearly comparable legislation was enacted in Scotland in **1988** before being repealed in 2000. In a separate incident, David Norris appealed his case (Norris v. Ireland) to the European Court of Human Rights after losing cases in the Irish High Court and Irish Supreme Court in 1980 and 1983 respectively. The Irish statute that made male-to-male intercourse illegal was overturned by the European Court on the grounds of privacy, while homosexuality remained unlawful in Ireland until 1993.

In **1991**, *Assembly Bill 101*, which forbade employers from discriminating against employees because of their sexual orientation, was vetoed by Pete Wilson, the state's then-governor, ultimately leading to the AB101 Veto Riot in California.

Despite winning support, the LGBT community in Nicaragua experienced a setback when social Christians in the National Assembly amended a bill that had been created to defend women from rape and sexual assault. As a result of the amendment, "anyone who induces, encourages, propagandizes, or engages in intercourse between members of the same sex in a scandalous manner" could face a term of up to three years in prison. Furthermore, all unmarried sexual acts were included. President Violeta Chamorro signed the measure into law as *Article 204* of the Nicaraguan Criminal Code in July **1992** amid protests from activists and their allies in Nicaragua and at foreign embassies.

Lesbians, bisexual women, homosexual men, and straight males were all prohibited from joining the military prior to the implementation of the *"Don't Ask, Don't Tell"* policy in **1993**. Despite the military being prohibited from inquiring about a service member's sexual orientation when the policy was put into effect, up to its repeal in 2011, service members were still subject to expulsion from the military if they had intercourse with someone of the same sex, came out as lesbian, gay, or bisexual, or had either wed or attempted to wed someone of the same sex.

While addressing a crowd of students in **1997**, Israeli President Ezer Weizman drew the analogy between alcoholism and homosexuality. This meant that students were made to believe that being LGBTQIA+ was at par with addiction.

On the evening of October 6, 1998, a gay American University of Wyoming student named Matthew Wayne Shepard was assaulted, tortured, and then left to die next to Laramie. Rescuers rushed him to Poudre Valley Hospital in Fort Collins, Colorado, where he succumbed to serious brain injuries he sustained during the assault six days later. In a separate instance, Rita Hester, an African-American transgender woman, was murdered on November 28, **1998**, in Allston, Massachusetts. Due to the outpouring of grief and rage following her death, a candlelight vigil was organized the following Friday (December 4), and roughly 250 people attended.

In **2002**, Volkert van der Graaf assassinated Dutch politician Pim Fortuyn, who was openly gay.

Homosexual behavior was once again criminalized in Belize in **2003**.

Australia, the US states of Mississippi, Missouri, Montana, Oregon, and Utah banned same-sex marriages, while Arkansas, Georgia, Kentucky, Louisiana, Michigan, North Dakota, Ohio, Oklahoma, Virginia, and Wisconsin were US states that banned same-sex civil unions and marriages in **2004**.

In **2005**, same-sex unions were banned in Latvia, Uganda, and Honduras, while Kansas and Texas were American states that banned same-sex marriages and civil unions. In the same year, Mahmoud Asgari and Ayaz Marhoni, two homosexual male teens, were executed in Iran; and a directive from the Roman Catholic Church asserted that anybody with "deep-seated homosexual tendencies" or who "supports the so-called 'gay culture'" was not eligible to become a priest. This statement by the Church was a bit odd considering that they say priesthood is a "calling from God" to this very day.

In **2006**, the US State of Tennessee banned same-sex marriages, while Alabama, Colorado, Idaho, South Carolina, South Dakota, Virginia, and Wisconsin banned same-sex unions and marriages. Kentucky, a state in the United States, overturned its anti-discrimination statutes in the same year, while the *Federal Marriage Amendment* was rejected by the US Senate. The maiden Moscow gay pride march witnessed intense violence as it concluded.

In the year **2008**, Arizona, Maine and California in the US were the states that banned same-sex marriages, while Florida banned same-sex unions and marriages. Additionally, Arkansas banned same-sex adoption (struck down by the Arkansas Supreme Court in 2011). In Greeley, Colorado, a transgender woman named Angie Zapata was murdered. Since he killed her after discovering she was transgender, Allen Andrade was found guilty of first-degree murder and a crime motivated by prejudice. A conviction for a hate crime involving a transgender victim was obtained in this instance for the first time in the country. On November 1ˢᵗ, 2009, *"Aqui y Ahora"* on Univision portrayed the life and murder of Angie Zapata.

In **2013**, India reinstated its anti-homosexuality laws by overturning the 2009 Delhi High Court judgment on *Section 377*. In the same year, federal legislation prohibiting the dissemination of "propaganda of non-traditional sexual relations" to minors was enacted by the Russian government. The use of the internet or the media to encourage "non-traditional relationships" was punishable by severe fines under the law.

In **2014**, eleven African countries strengthened their laws on sodomy, while homosexuality was a punishable offense in Brunei, and same-sex marriages were prohibited in Nigeria.

Conservative US states started passing "religious liberty" legislation in **2015**, permitting discrimination against LGBTQ people based on their religious beliefs.

To stop transgender people from using public facilities that correspond to their gender identification, conservative U.S. states began introducing "bathroom bills" in **2016**.

In **2017**, homosexuality was deemed a criminal offense in Chad via *Article 354* and *Article 360* of the penal code. Former Prime Minister Delwa Kassiré Coumakoye stated a religious rationale in favor of the criminalizing law that was implemented saying, "Homosexuality is condemned by all religions. We do not have to forgive something that God himself rejects because Westerners have said this or that."

While Brunei toughened its sodomy laws to punish homosexuality with death by stoning in **2019**, Gabon made homosexuality a criminal offense before repealing the statute a year later.

In the United States, conservative states started passing legislation to restrict transgender girls and women from participating in school sports in **2020**, while Russia's constitution banned same-sex marriages.

The *"Don't Say Gay"* legislation in Florida in **2022** forbade the mention or representation of LGBT individuals in elementary (and possibly higher grade) schools.

It is undeniable from this glimpse into the past that deliberate efforts were made to ensure that LGBTQIA+ individuals ceased to exist. Even some convicts who have committed the most heinous crimes were given the opportunity to live with dignity, but our community was treated far worse than felons. Violence seems to have been the dominant motif in the past, where the elected "leaders" of their respective nations advocated violence over compassion. It has been formerly suggested that we should shape the future by drawing lessons from the past, however, it appears that the disturbing historical scenarios continue to be repeatedly emulated to this day. It is unsettling that despite evidence of oppression, our existence is still declared to be rather "relatively new." Do you agree with the claim?

I would like you to reflect on a couple of questions before we proceed any further:

1. Do you believe that someone who just loves another person, connects with their innate physiology, or simply lives their life on their terms should have to go through such suffering?
2. Are the historical tragedies that robbed us of our basic human rights, tormented us without consequence, and dehumanized us justified?

CHAPTER THREE

EVIDENCE OF EXISTENCE AND CELEBRATION

Throughout history, our community has transcended persecution while always leaving its mark. From representation in carvings on rocks to the works of artists across genres and legislation that recognized same-sex marriages, let us dive into the momentous events that highlighted the quiddity of the LGBTQIA+ community, in case the horrendous episodes in the previous chapter weren't sufficient to prove its interminable existence.

The phallic male figures in pairs that were carved in Sicilian Mesolithic rock art between **c. 9,600 – c. 5,000 BCE** have been variably interpreted as portrayals of male gay intercourse, acrobats, hunters, and religious initiates.

In the prehistoric San rock drawings of Zimbabwe, Africa, homosexuality was first represented to the world in **8000 BCE**.

An example of a "third sex" human figure with female breasts and male genitalia or without recognizable sex traits could be seen in Neolithic and Bronze Age artwork and sculptures from the Mediterranean region between **c. 7,000 – c. 1700 BCE**. Female pictures were prevalent in household contexts in Neolithic Italy, whereas images that mix sexual features were found in tombs or religious settings. Figures from Neolithic Greece and Cyprus were frequently shown as dual-sexed or without identifiable sexual traits.

In **3100 BCE**, Arjuna spent a year as a crossdressing transsexual and was welcomed at King Virata's court, according to the Indian epic the *Mahabharata*.

A male was buried in the attire typically worn by ladies in a cemetery in a Prague suburb between **c. 2900 – c. 2500 BCE**. Archaeologists think the grave belonged to a transgender person or a third-sex individual.

The fabled Chinese Emperor Huang Di, who was said to have had male lovers in **2697 BCE**, was not the first ancient governing monarch in Chinese history to have done so.

In **c. 2400 BCE**,the first same-sex pair in recorded history was believed to be Khnumhotep and Niankhkhnum.

Between **2284 – 2246 or 2184 BCE**, Pepi II Neferkare, known as the Pharaoh of Egypt, ruled the Kingdom of Egypt as an absolute king and was rumored to have had homosexual tendencies based on his nighttime visits to his General Sasenet.

A gay union between the two gods was described in *The Contendings of Horus and Seth*, a document from early Middle Kingdom Egypt, around the year **2040 BCE**.

It was recorded that King Zimri-Lim of the Kingdom of Mari had male lovers during his reign between **c. 1775 – c. 1761 BCE**.

A literature from India's Vedic Period, the *Shatapatha Brahmana*, depicted a homosexual marriage between the brother-gods Mitra and Varuna in the year **800 BCE**. Greek epics from the eighth century, such as the *Iliad* and *Odyssey*, depicted gay relationships between deities and young men, including Zeus and Ganymede, Poseidon and Pelops, Apollo and Hyacinth, and others.

The first Greek record of the social institution of paiderastia was an inscription from Crete in **c. 630 BCE**. Dorian aristocracy in Crete adopted formal relationships between adult aristocrats and adolescent boys. While it was illegal for males to be married in Greece, they could establish committed partnerships called paiderastia ("pederasty," without the pejorative connotations of the English word). These relationships resembled heterosexual marriages with the exception that the older person served as a mentor or tutor.

Between **630 – 612 BCE**, the island of Lesbos gave birth to the Greek lyric poet Sappho, who passed away around 570 BCE. She was one of the nine lyric poets listed by the Alexandrians. She gained notoriety for her lesbian themes and contributed to the concept of lesbianism by using her name and that of her own country (and the lesser-used term "sapphism").

The *Pali Canon*, which documented the words of Gautama Buddha, was written between **600 – 100 BCE**. It stated that sexual relations, whether homosexual or heterosexual in nature, were forbidden in the monastic code and that any acts of soft homosexual sex (such as masturbation and interfumeral sex), while not punishable, had to be confessed to the monastery. Only monks were subject to these laws; the general public was not. While being predominantly composed in Sri Lanka, the *Pali*

Canon was based on the writings of Buddha in India.

Homosexual liaisons were seen in wall paintings from the Etruscan Tomb of the Bulls (Italian: Tomba dei Tori) between **c. 540 – 530 BCE**, which were discovered in the Monterozzi necropolis, Tarquinia, in 1892. The tomb is named after a pair of bulls that are depicted watching human sex acts, one involving a man and a woman and the other involving two men. These acts may be apotropaic or represent the afterlife and the cycle of regeneration. The three-chamber tomb's inscription included the name of the deceased, Aranth Spurianas or Arath Spuriana, as well as a depiction of Achilles slaying the Trojan prince Troilus and indications of an Apollo cult.

According to the Hindu epic *Ramayana*, Hanuman witnessed two homosexuals having a sexual encounter on the island of Lanka in **500 BCE**.

In **c. 440 BCE**, when Herodotus published *Histories*, he said that Persians embraced foreign practices and did so by embracing pederasty, a Greek custom.

The *Sushruta Samhita*, an ancient Indian medical treatise, classified gay, transgender, and intersex conditions as inborn and incurable in **400 BCE**. In order to help satisfy the libido of affluent Greeks, historian Herodotus recounted Middle Eastern slave dealers selling castrated adolescents at Sardis. Castrating a male was seen as "undignified, with just a few exceptions," he stated.

In **385 BCE**, Phaedrus, Eryximachus, Aristophanes, and other Greek intellectuals argue in Plato's *Symposium* that sex with women is lustful and utilitarian whereas love between men is the purest kind. But Socrates is an exception. He exhibits extraordinary restraint when Alcibiades, who is attractive, seduces him.

The soldiers of Philip II of Macedon annihilated the Sacred Band of Thebes in **338 BCE**, a hitherto unbeaten elite regiment made up of 150 pederastic couples. Philip bemoaned their loss and honored them.

Bagoas, a favored catamite of King Darius III, became the catamite of King Alexander III of Macedon in **330 BCE**.

Initiation ceremonies for the Greek Cybele worship took place in **200 BCE**, during which males castrated themselves voluntarily, dressed like women, and took on feminine names and identities.

Homosexuals were included among the males who are infertile with women in India's *Narada-smriti* around **100 BCE**, and they were also deemed incurable and ineligible for marriage to people of the opposite sex. One of the first records of homosexuality could be found in the Celtic tribes of northern Gaul and Britannia, according to Roman historian Diodorus Siculus.

In the latter years of the Republic, a group of poets led by Quintus Lutatius Catulus made short, lyrical Hellenistic poems fashionable between the **c. 90s – 80s BCE**. His two surviving epigrams that speak to a man as the object of desire signaled the emergence of a new homoerotic aesthetic in Roman society.

Between **57 – 54 BCE**, *Carmina* was written by Catullus, who boasted of his sexual ability with young people in his love poems to Juventius and in his furious invectives against "passive" homosexuals.

In **44 BCE**, Gaius Octavius was officially identified in Gaius Julius Caesar's testament as his adoptive son and successor after the assassination of the dictator and consul. Octavius had procured his adoption by Caesar through sexual favors, according to Mark Antony's accusation.

The *Eclogues* was written by Virgil between **42 – 39 BCE**, and Eclogue 2 was considered a noteworthy work of homoerotic Latin literature.

Augustus established the Roman Empire in **27 BCE**. During his rule, the first official same-sex marriage took place.

Castration was prohibited across the whole Roman Empire in **0 CE**, or the first century.

In the early Roman Empire between **c. 1 – 5 CE**, transgender persons were described by Philo of Alexandria and Marcus Manilius. According to Philo, "Expending all effort on their outer ornamentation, they are not embarrassed even to use every method to alter their essence as males into women artificially." He also confirmed that a number of the group's members had their penises removed for that purpose.

The Warren Cup, a Roman silver drinking cup featuring two relief depictions of same-sex male actions, was created between **5 – 15 CE**.

After Nero was crowned as the Emperor of Rome in **54 CE**, he legally wed Pythagoras and Sporus, giving Sporus the regalia used by the wives of the Caesars. Juvenal and Martial remarked with disdain that male couples were having conventional marriage rituals.

In **79 CE**, a vast collection of Roman sexual art, including images of male-male and female-female, was preserved when Mount Vesuvius erupted, burying the seaside resorts of Pompeii and Herculaneum.

One of the most adored Roman emperors, Trajan, ascended to the throne in **98 CE**. Trajan was well-known for his homosexuality and affection for young males. Abgar VII, King of Edessa, had angered Trajan because for some reason, and took advantage of this by sending his gorgeous young son to apologize and win Trajan's forgiveness.

The Greek moralist Plutarch wrote of Heracles' (Hercules') numerous male lovers around the year **100 CE**. These men included Apollo, Aberus, a number of the Argonauts, Nestor, Iolaos, and an untold number of others.

The reign of the Roman emperor Elagabalus commenced between **218 – 222 CE**, and at various points during his reign, Elagabalus married five women as well as an athlete from Smyrna named Zoticus in a lavish public ceremony in Rome. However, the Syrian's most committed relationship was with the charioteer Hierocles, and according to Cassius Dio, Elagabalus enjoyed being referred to as Hierocles' mistress, wife, and queen. The emperor was indeed viewed by some writers as an early transgender figure and one of the first individuals on record to seek sex reassignment surgery as they claim that they wore makeup and wigs, preferred to be addressed as a lady rather than a lord, and offered sizable sums to any doctor who could give them a vagina.

The *Kama Sutra* was written in **300 CE**, during the affluent Gupta Dynasty of India. The famed work extensively addressed gay behavior and individuals, referring to them as a third nature or sex (tritiya-prakriti). Tamil Sangam literature from the same year discussed partnerships between two men and delved into the lives of trans women in the Aravan cult in the Tamil Nadu hamlet of Koovagam.

Sergius and Bacchus, two Roman commanders, were executed in Syria in **303 CE** for preaching Christianity. They were eventually declared saints and served as a role model for same-sex unions and "wedded brotherhood" rituals that were practiced in Christian societies from the seventh through the eighteenth centuries.

Constans I and Constantius II ascended to the position of Roman Emperor in **337 CE**. Both of them were involved in same-sex relationships when they were in power.

Between **390 – 405** CE*Dionysiaca* by Nonnus was the last known work of Western literature to honor gay ardor in over a millennium.

The LGBT community today has adopted Anastasia the Patrician as an example of a "transgender" saint after she quit her position as a lady-in-waiting at Justinian I's court in Constantinople to spend twenty-eight years in isolation in Egypt while clothed as a male monk until her death in **576 CE**.

Following the establishment of the Abbasid Caliphate in **c. 750 CE**, Muslim poets such as the Persian-Arab poet Abu Nuwas began to write homoerotic poems directed towards attractive youth.

Traditional Norse myths and customs, some of which include gay behavior and cross-dressing, were documented in literature in **800 CE**.

Between **800 – 900 CE**, Alcuin of York, an abbot, penned love poems to other monks during the Carolingian Renaissance despite the fact that there were numerous Church regulations against homosexuality at the time.

Castrating homosexual house workers and slaves became common practice in northern India around the year **1000** courtesy of Muslims who arrived there in the eleventh century.

On the Indian subcontinent, temple building flourished in the year 1000, and some of them were decorated with overtly erotic depictions of homosexuality.

In the Kingdom of León, a chapel served as the venue for the marriage of Pedro Dias and Muo Vandilas which is officiated by a priest in **1061**.

In **1100**, Ivo of Chartres tried to persuade Pope Urban II of the dangers of homosexuality. Ivo accused the archbishop of Tours, Rodolfo, of influencing the French monarch to install a certain Giovanni as the bishop of Orléans. The monarch publicly boasted about the fact that Giovanni was well known as Rodolfo's lover and had intercourse with him. But, Pope Urban did not view this as a decisive fact. Rodolfo remained to be well-known and revered during Giovanni's almost forty-year tenure as bishop. In his book, *Defense of Eunuchs*, published in 1100, Archbishop Theophylaktos presented a defense for eunuchs as a significant social class that contributed to Byzantine culture. The Prophet Mohammed's tomb in Medina was guarded by eunuchs sometime in the twelfth or earlier century.

De spiritali amicitia, written by the English monk Aelred of Rievaulx in **1164**, gave love between individuals of the same gender a profound expression.

It is claimed that a red-hot poker was used to murder the overthrown King Edward II of England in **1327**. The nobles and Edward II had a troubled relationship in the past because they frequently exiled the Lord of Cornwall, Piers Gaveston, his former lover.

In **1347**, the trial of Rolandino Roncaglia for sodomy made headlines throughout Italy. He acknowledged that "neither with his wife nor with any other woman, he had ever had sexual intercourse, since he had never had any carnal appetite, nor could he ever have an erection of his virile organ." After his wife passed away from the plague, Rolandino began to prostitute himself while dressed as a woman since "many people regarded him to be a woman due to his looks," despite the fact that he "had a male member and testicles, but had a feminine look, voice, and mannerisms."

Under the new Islamic ruler, Mehmet II, the Ottoman Turks conquered the Byzantine Empire in **1453**, and attitudes toward homosexuality improved.

The infant Nimai (Sri Caitanya Mahaprabhu), a significant incarnation of Radha and Krishna, was blessed by transgender dancers in Bengal, India, around **1486**.

While staying at a monastery near Steyn, the Netherlands, Desiderius Erasmus composed a string of love letters for a fellow monk in **1492**. Christopher Columbus discovered the New World in the same year while looking for a quicker way to India.

Conquistador Hernando Cortez recorded rampant homosexuality among the Veracruz people of Mexico in a report to King Carlos V of Spain in **1519**.

Conquistador Francisco Pizarro of Spain provided in-depth accounts of sodomy and transvestite ceremonies carried out by Incan priests and chieftains in **1528**.

Around 300 love poems by Michelangelo, a Florentine artist, were written for Tomasso degli Cavalieri in **1532**.

In **1542**, *The Journey of Alvar Nuñez Cabeza de Vaca and His Companions from Florida to the Pacific 1528–1536* by Alvar Nuñez Cabeza de Vaca documented same-sex unions and males "who dress like women and do the office of women, but use the bow and carry big loads" among a Native American tribe.

A number of court documents from Portugal's Brazil colony between **1591 – 1593** included one of the oldest reports of homosexuality in Africa, describing sodomitic activities among the indigenous of Angola and the Congo.

A group of native Africans in Portuguese Angola known as chibados, who dressed as women, married other men, and "esteeme that unnaturale damnation an honor", was described in a **1625** document by Jesuit priest Joao dos Santos.

Thomasine Hall, an intersex woman, was ordered by a perplexed colonial American court in **1629** to wear both male and female attire.

The widely regarded intersex or lesbian Christina Alexandra was proclaimed Queen of Sweden in **1633**.

Dutch officers Caron and Schouten reported in **1636** that Japanese Buddhist nobility and monks openly embraced sodomy.

Francisco Coreal, a traveler and writer from Spain, described a group of "hermaphrodite" boys who dressed like women and engaged in sodomy with the local males in Florida in **1669**.

Robert de La Salle claimed France's ownership over the Louisiana Territory in **1682**. Early French explorers in Quebec, Louisiana, and the Great Lakes saw homosexual native crossdressers and gave them the name "berdache."

The first Japanese homosexual club, Kagemachaya(ja), opened in Japan between **1688 – 1704**.

Dutchman Engelbert Kaempfer observed the prevalence of transgender Kabuki dancers who performed as boy prostitutes throughout Japan in **1691**.

One of the earliest known German homosexuals, Frederick II the Great, was anointed King of Prussia in **1740**.

Captain James Cook observed that the Maori tribes of New Zealand embraced homosexuality in **1770**. Across all of the South Seas, similar observations were made by European explorers.

Gustav III, who was popularly believed to be gay, was crowned King of Sweden in **1771**.

Thomas Jefferson drafted a statute in **1778** that called for castration as an alternative to hanging for sodomy, however the Virginia Legislature rejected the proposal.

In **1785**, Jeremy Bentham became one of the pioneers in the fight to decriminalize sodomy in England.

In **1791**, *The French Penal Code of 1791*, which no longer considered sodomy to be a crime, was adopted by the Kingdom of France (including Andorra and Haiti). As a result, France became the first nation in Western Europe to legalize homosexual activities carried out by consenting adults. in the same year, China saw the publication of Cao Xueqin's novel *Dream of the Red Chamber*, which featured a character who was openly bisexual and an account of gay bashing. A Cuban newspaper story from the same year decried the "effeminate sodomites" who allegedly flourished in Havana in the eighteenth century. In the same year, homosexuality was made legal in the French Indian territories of Pondicherry.

In the year **1793**, sodomy had been made legal in Monaco.

The death sentence for sodomy was abolished in the Kingdom of Prussia in **1794**. Sodomy was also no longer considered a criminal offense in Luxembourg that same year.

Belgian legislation rendered sodomy legal in **1795**.

In **1802**, Piedmont was annexed by the French Republic, resulting in the extension of the *French Penal Code of 1791* to the acquired territory.

In his book *Travels in China* from **1806**, the English explorer John Barrow wrote of the sodomy he experienced among Hong Kong authorities.

In **1807**, The Duchy of Warsaw was established, which reinstated the legality of same-sex relationships. In the same year, Charity Bryant and Sylvia Drake, two Vermont residents, began dating and became one of the first documented same-sex couples in American history. The 2014 book *Charity and Sylvia: A Same-Sex Marriage in Early America* by historian Rachel Hope Cleves provided the most comprehensive documentation of this relationship.

The *Napoleonic Code* was extended to the annexed region when the French Empire annexed the States of the Church in **1809**. Blasphemy, heresy, sacrilege, witchcraft, incest, and homosexuality were not mentioned in the Napoleonic Code, which prompted their speedy decriminalization.

In **1811**, the *Napoleonic Code* was extended to the annexed territory when the French Empire annexed the German North Sea coast, while the Netherlands abolished legislation that rendered homosexual behavior illegal.

The *Napoleonic Code* was extended to Catalonia as a result of the French Empire's annexation of the region in **1812**.

In **1813**, laws outlawing homosexual activity between consenting adults were abolished in the Kingdom of Bavaria.

In **1822**, homosexuality was no longer a crime in the Dominican Republic, and it was made legal in El Salvador.

The Brazilian Empire decriminalized homosexuality in **1830**.

Homosexuality was no longer considered a criminal offense in Bolivia in **1832**.

Laws criminalizing gay activity between consenting individuals were repealed in Hannover in **1840**.

In Portugal, homosexual activities were no longer illegal in **1852**.

Argentina ended the criminalization of homosexuality in **1853**.

In **1856**, a Salt Lake City resident wrote in his notebook that a Mormon lady was "trying to entice a little girl," resulting in the first recorded mention of lesbians in Mormon history.

During the Tanzimat reform period, the Ottoman Empire, the country that eventually became Turkey, decriminalized homosexuality in **1858**.

Homosexuality was no longer a crime in San Marino in **1865**. In the same year, on August 29, as he advocated for a resolution demanding the repeal of anti-gay legislation at the Congress of German Jurists in Munich, Karl Heinrich Ulrichs became the first homosexual individual to openly defend homosexuality. He was yelled at to stop. According to Robert Beachy, it was appropriate to refer to Ulrichs as the first openly gay person, as he stated in an interview.

The term "homosexual" was first recognized in literature in a German pamphlet written by Austrian-born author Karl-Maria Kertbeny that was published in **1869** under an alias and argued against a Prussian anti-sodomy statute. In the same year, homosexuality was no longer considered to be unlawful in Suriname. In the same pamphlets that Karl-Maria Kertbeny used to argue against the Prussian sodomy statute and in which he first used the terms "homosexual" and "heterosexual," he also used the term "monosexuals" to describe those who exclusively engage in masturbation.

The novel *"Joseph and His Friend: A Story of Pennsylvania"* was published in **1870**, possibly making history as the first homosexual relationship fiction in the United States.

In **1871**, homosexuality was no longer a criminal offense in Guatemala and Mexico.

Anal sodomy, or homosexual activities, were only rendered illegal in the early Meiji Restoration era until they were decriminalized by the Japanese Empire in **1880**. In the same year, homosexuality was also no longer illegal in Paraguay.

In Italy and the Vatican, homosexuality was made legal in **1890**.

The translation of Kraft-Ebing's *Psychopathia Sexualis* by Charles Gilbert Chaddock in **1892** marked the first time the terms "bisexual" and "heterosexual" were used in the English language in their contemporary senses. In the same year, Edna St. Vincent Millay, a well-known poet who was openly bisexual, was born on February 22.

Adolfo Caminha's controversial novel *Bom-Crioulo* (in English: The Black Man and the Cabin Boy) was published in Brazil in **1895**, with homosexuality at its core and a Black man as the story's hero.

Magnus Hirschfeld, a German sexologist, highlighted those who lack sexual desire and connected them to the idea of "anesthesia sexual" in his **1896** booklet *Sappho and Sokrates*.

Magnus Hirschfeld initiated a lifelong campaign for the repeal of *Paragraph 175* in December **1897** by petitioning the Reichstag. In the same year, Order of Chaeronea, the first homosexual rights organization in England, was founded by George Cecil Ives. In her book *Ein Weib? Psychologisch-biographische: Studie über eine Konträrsexuelle* (A woman? Psychological-biographical study of a contrary-sexual), German sexual reformer Emma Trosse also provided the first description of asexuality, under the label Sinnlichkeitslosigkeit (Asensuality). She also self-dentified using the same label by stating in her work that "verfasser hat den Mut, sich zu jener Kategorie zu bekennen (author has the courage to admit to this category)."

Homosexuality was no longer considered a violation of law in Honduras in **1899**.

Elisa Sanchez Loriga and Marcela Gracia Ibeas attempted to wed on June 8, **1901**, in A Coruña, Galicia, Spain. In order to do so, Elisa had to assume the identity of the man, Mario Sanchez, which was listed on the marriage license.

Karl M. Baer underwent sex reassignment surgery in December **1906**, making him the first transgender person to undergo the procedure. *Imre*, possibly the first openly homosexual novel with a happy ending in America, was published in the same year.

Emma Goldman made her first public remarks in support of LGBT rights in **1910**. Later, Magnus Hirschfeld noted that "she was the first and only woman, in fact, the first and only American, to take up the defense of homosexual love before the general public."

When the *"Young Woman's Journal"* paid homage to "Sappho of Lesbos" in **1912**, it became the first explicit mention of lesbianism in a Mormon publication. In the same year, Dr. Jacob Schorer founded the Scientific Humanitarian Committee of the Netherlands (NWHK), the first Dutch organization to combat anti-homosexual prejudice.

The former penal code, including *Article 995*, was entirely repealed in Russia after the October Revolution in **1917**. Homosexual partnerships and heterosexual relationships were considered precisely the same by the law, according to Bolshevik leaders.

In **1919**, Doctor Magnus Hirschfeld partnered in the establishment of the Institut für Sexualwissenschaft (Institute for Sex Research), a ground-breaking private research facility and counseling center, in Berlin, Germany. That same year, one of the first explicitly homosexual movies, *Different from the Others*, was published, and Magnus Hirschfeld appeared in the movie and contributed to its funding.

An effort to outlaw lesbianism in England for the first time in British history was unsuccessful in **1921**.

In the USSR, a new criminal legislation was enacted decriminalizing homosexual activities in **1922**. *The Female Impersonators*, a book about sexual and gender nonconformity by American author Jennie June, was published in 1922. June refers to those who lack sexual desire as "anaphrodites" in the article. June said that, "Because they don't believe in heroes, the idea of any association based on sex differences makes them violently shudder. Their anaphroditism is either hereditary or a result of a childhood disease". Immanuel Kant and Sir Isaac Newton "appear to have been anaphrodites", June adds.

In **1923**, Elsa Gidlow, a lesbian who was born in England, published *On a Grey Thread*, the first collection of openly lesbian love poetry in the United States.

Henry Gerber established the Society for Human Rights in Chicago in **1924**, which was the nation's first organization dedicated to gay rights. A few months passed before the gang disbanded as a result of police harassment. In the same year, both Peru and Paraguay made homosexuality legal.

The New York Times was the first significant media outlet to use the word homosexuality in **1926**.

In **1927**, Karol Szymanowski, Poland's openly homosexual composer, had been named director of the Fryderyk Chopin Music Academy, Poland's state-owned national music institution.

Radclyffe Hall's *The Well of Loneliness* was first released in the UK and then in the United States in **1928**. As a result, there was intense legal debate, and homosexuality became a major topic of discussion.

The first known LGBT protest in history was organized by Las Carolinas in **1931**. They were a group of transvestites from Barcelona and they did this in response to the destruction of a popular LGBT gathering spot in Barcelona (Catalonia, Spain), a central public bath. In the same year, the first explicitly lesbian and pro-lesbian movie, *Mädchen in Uniform*, was published, and Dora Richter underwent vaginoplasty in Berlin, making her the first transgender woman to do so.

In Poland, the legal age of consent for both homosexuals and heterosexuals was codified to be 15 in **1932**. Although prohibited in 1835 by the occupying forces, homosexuality was never a criminal offense under Polish law.

In **1933**, homosexuality was no longer illegal under the new *Danish Penal Code*.

Uruguay officially decriminalized homosexuality in **1934**.

Mona's 440 Club, the first lesbian club in America, debuted in San Francisco in **1936**. Mona's servers and female entertainers donned tuxedos, while the patrons dressed in character.

The pink triangle was first used in Nazi concentration camps by homosexual men in **1937**.

When referring to homosexuality, the word "gay" was used for the first time in **1938** in the motion picture

Bringing Up Baby.

The first explicitly lesbian autobiography in which two women find happiness together was *Diana: A Strange Autobiography,* which was written by Frances V. Rummell in **1939**. She was a teacher of French at Stephens College, and this autobiography was released with a statement noting that the publishers wished it was understood expressly that this was a true story and was the first of its type to be made available to the general reading audience.

Homosexuality was no longer illegal in Iceland in **1940**.

The term "transsexuality" was first employed to refer to homosexuality and bisexuality in **1941**.

Switzerland decriminalized homosexuality in **1942**, with the consent age fixed at 20.

The poet Robert Duncan was the first well-known American to come out as gay. This occurred when he claimed that homosexuals were an oppressed minority in the anarchist magazine *Politics* in **1944** while writing under his own name. In the same year, Sweden and Suriname decriminalized homosexuality and established the consent age at 18 years old.

In the summer of **1945**, the first homosexual bar in post-World War II Berlin opened, and in the fall of the same year, the first drag gala was held in West Berlin's American district. In the same year, Yanagi, a gay pub, debuted in Japan, and the Veterans Benevolent Society was founded in the United States by four homosexual servicemen who had received honorable discharges.

In **1946**, one of the first homophile groups was established in the Netherlands and went by the abbreviation "COC" (Center for Culture and Recreation). It is the oldest Gay group still operating. In the same year, Michael Dillon underwent sex reassignment surgery in

London under the care of plastic surgeon Harold Gillies.

Between **1947 – 1948**, Lisa Ben, whose real name was Edith Eyde, developed and self-published *Vice Versa* in Los Angeles, the first lesbian publication in the United States.

A homosexual organization called "Forbundet af 1948" (the "League of 1948") was founded in Denmark in **1948**. The age of consent for all sexual acts, whether gay or heterosexual, was set at 15 by the communist government of Poland in the same year. According to study, 1.5% of adult male participants fell under category "X" on the Kinsey Scale in the same year, which was for males who reported no socio-sexual encounters or reactions.

By voluntarily undergoing sex reassignment surgery in **1950**, Rina Natan became the first transgender woman in Israel to do so. In the same year, Sweden saw the formation of the Organization for Sexual Equality, which is today known as the Swedish Federation for Lesbian, Gay, Bisexual and Transgender Rights (RFSL). Furthermore, the Nazi emendations to *Paragraph 175* were partially revoked by East Germany, and the Mattachine Society, the first active gay organization in the United States, was established in Los Angeles on 11 November.

With the age of consent established at 16, the *Jordanian Criminal Code* was revised in **1951**, legalizing private, adult, non-commercial, and consensual sodomy. Greece also saw the decriminalization of homosexuality in that same year.

The first lesbian paperback novel, *Spring Fire*, which marked the start of the lesbian pulp fiction subgenre, was released in **1952** and sold 1.5 million copies. Using the fictitious name Vin Packer, it was written by the lesbian author Marijane Meaker. As the first person with extensive media coverage to undergo sex reassignment surgery in the same year, Christine Jorgensen became a global sensation after receiving surgery to transition her gender from male to female. Moreover, with writer Yukio Mishima as a contributor, the male gay publication *"Adonis"* was launched in Japan.

On March 19, **1953**, a small group of friends in Houston, Texas, established The Diana Foundation. The Diana Foundation is a charity that holds two yearly fundraising events, including the Diana Awards, and is acknowledged as the oldest continually operating LGBT organization in the United States. According to the research, 19% of female interviewees in 1953 who took the Kinsey Scale survey fell into the category "X," which was for females who reported no socio-sexual encounters or reactions.

In **1954**, Arcadie was established as France's first LGBT organization.

The Daughters of Bilitis (DOB), the first national lesbian political and social organization in the United States, was established in San Francisco in **1955** by four lesbian couples, including Del Martin and Phyllis Lyon. The name of the ensemble was inspired by Pierre Louÿs' *Songs of Bilitis*, a song cycle with a lesbian theme that featured the mythical Bilitis as an inhabitant of the Isle of Lesbos alongside Sappho. In addition to conducting research, DOB's activities included organizing open forums on homosexuality, providing assistance to lone, married, and lesbian mothers, and supporting isolated lesbians. New York City's chapter of the Mattachine Society was established in the same year.

In the US, *The Ladder*, the first lesbian publication with national distribution, began publishing in **1956**. In the same year, homosexual activities were no longer illegal in Thailand.

American doctor Harry Benjamin was credited with coining the term "transsexual" in **1957**. According to the Wolfenden Committee's results of a study, the UK was recommended to decriminalize adults engaging in consensual homosexual behavior in the same year. Moreover, a key contributing reason to the American Psychiatric Association's decision to remove homosexuality from its list of disorders in 1973 was the publication of research by psychologist Evelyn Hooker demonstrating that gay men were as well adjusted as non-homosexual men. Also, Tom of Finland, a homoerotic artist, debuted on the cover of the Los Angeles-based *Physique Pictorial* magazine.

The first decision of the U.S. Supreme Court to deal with homosexuality and the first to discuss free speech rights with regard to homosexuality was One, Inc. v. Olesen, 355 U.S. 371 in **1958**. The Supreme Court upheld the constitutional protection for pro-homosexual expression by overturning a lower court's ruling that the gay periodical ONE magazine had violated obscenity statutes. The UK served as the birthplace of the Homosexual Law Reform Society that same year. Furthermore, the Daughters of Bilitis' New York chapter was established by Barbara Gittings. The Gold Coast, the country's first gay leather bar established by Dom Orejudos and Chuck Renslow, debuted in Chicago in the same year.

In **1959**, ITV, the sole national commercial broadcaster in the UK at the time, broadcasted *South*, the country's first homosexual TV drama starring Peter Wyngarde.

In **1960**, the first lesbians to successfully fight their dismissal from the U.S. military for being homosexual were Cpls. Fannie Mae Clackum and Grace Garner, U.S. Air Force reservists in the late 1940s and early 1950s. The decision hinged on the lack of sufficient evidence to support the women's lesbian identities.

Victim, which had its UK debut on August 31, **1961**, was the first English-language movie to use the term "homosexual." In the same year, sodomy was no longer considered an offense in Hungary. Furthermore, *The Rejected*, the first homosexuality-related documentary to air on American television, debuted on KQED TV in San Francisco on September 11. Also, by running for the San Francisco Board of Supervisors, José Sarria made history as the nation's first openly homosexual politician.

In response to ongoing police harassment and the closing of gay bars (including the Tay-Bush Inn raid), gay bar owners founded The Tavern Guild, the first gay business association in the United States, in **1962**. The organization lasted until 1995. In the same year, via the adoption of the American Law Institute's *Model Penal Code*, Illinois becomes the very first U.S. state to eliminate the sodomy law from its criminal code. Although not criminalizing private carnal relations, the adopted law did make "Open Lewdness" a crime. Furthermore, sodomy was no longer a crime in Czechoslovakia, and the Dorian Society, the first homosexual men's group in New Zealand, was established and operated from 1962 until 1988.

In Philadelphia, the regional Daughters of Bilitis, Janus Society, and Mattachine Society chapters came together to create the East Coast Homophile Organizations (ECHO) in **1963**. In the same year, by means of a judicial decision against the implementation of the relevant clause of the old British-mandate statute from 1936 (which was never enforced), Israel de facto decriminalized sodomy and male-to-male sexual activity.

Ted Northe established the "Imperial Court of Canada," a monarchist organization made up mostly of drag performers, in March **1964**. This organization served as a catalyst for the country's movement toward equality. Being the oldest continually operating LGBT organization in Canada, The Courts of Canada have over 14 chapters across the nation. In the same year, ASK was Canada's first gay-positive organization, and *Gay*, published by the Gay Publishing Company in Toronto, and *ASK Newsletter*, in Vancouver were the country's first homosexual magazines. *Gay* was the first periodical to incorporate the word "Gay" in the title, and it immediately outgrew the reach of American periodicals published under the moniker *Gay International*. *Two* (published by the Toronto-based Gayboy (later Kamp) Publishing Company) quickly followed these. In September, a shot of two women standing back-to-back on a beach and gazing out to sea appeared on the front cover of the lesbian journal *The Ladder*. Furthermore, the first time a major newspaper covered LGBT concerns was in the June 1964 Paul Welch *Life* article *Homosexuality in America*. Also, the Council on Religion and the Homosexual was the first organization in the United States to include the word "homosexual" in its name when it was established in the same year.

On July 4, **1965**, homosexuals and lesbians protested outside Independence Hall in Philadelphia while wearing conservative clothing. This was the first of several Annual Reminders that were held throughout 1969. In the same year, a forum for local politicians to answer questions about issues affecting gay and lesbian persons, such as police intimidation, was hosted by the Council on Religion and the Homosexual. This was the first time "the gay vote" was allegedly sought for. Furthermore, the LGBT youth group

Vanguard was founded in the impoverished Tenderloin district. It is regarded as the United States' first gay liberation group.

Lilli Vincenz was the first lesbian to have her face displayed on the cover of the lesbian journal *The Ladder* in January **1966**. The Mattachine Society organized a "Sip-In" at Julius Bar in New York City that same year to protest a law passed by the New York State Liquor Authority prohibiting the distribution of alcohol to homosexuals. Furthermore, the National Planning Conference of Homophile Organizations was formed, and later that year it changed its name to NACHO (North American Conference of Homophile Organizations). As a means to protest the exclusion of LGBT people from the U.S. armed forces, a coalition of homosexual organizations organized protests on Armed Forces Day. The first gay pride parade in the country was a 15-car motorcade that was organized in Los Angeles in the same year. The National Transsexual Counseling Unit was also founded, making it the first transgender organization worldwide and the first transgender organization in the United States. Lastly, the first gay and lesbian community center in America was established by the Society for Individual Rights.

The first network documentary to address the subject of homosexuality was an episode of CBS Reports from **1967** titled *The Homosexuals*. England and Wales officially decriminalized homosexuality, courtesy of the *Sexual Offences Act 1967*, while Scotland, Northern Ireland, and the Channel Islands were exempt from the law. Greater Buenos Aires witnessed the founding of Grupo Nuestro Mundo (English: "Our World Group"), the first LGBT rights group in Argentina and Latin America. *The Advocate* was first released as *The Los Angeles Advocate* in September and was a local newsletter informing homosexual men about police raids on gay establishments in Los Angeles. In the same year, Wainwright Churchill's book *Homosexual Behavior Among Males* pioneered the field of scientific study into homosexuality as a reality and popularized the word "homoerotophobia," which is believed to be a forerunner of the term "homophobia." Furthermore, the first bookshop in the world with a gay focus, the Oscar Wilde Bookstore, opened in New York City, and the Student Homophile League at Columbia University became the country's first institutionally-recognized LGBT student organization.

In **1968**, Bulgaria decriminalized homosexuality, while in East Germany, homosexuality was made legal by virtue of *Paragraph 175*. In the wake of the Compton riot, the National Transsexual Counseling Unit (NTCU), the network's apex of transgender social, psychological, and medical support services, was founded that same year, becoming the first peer-run support and advocacy organization in the world. The Patch (an LGBT bar) owner Lee Glaze gathered the other customers to march on the police station in Los Angeles after two customers were detained during a raid. After taking over a neighboring flower shop, the protesters caravanned to the station, decorated it with flowers, and released the guys who had been taken into custody.

By enacting *Bill C-150*, Canada decriminalized homosexuality in **1969**. According to a statement from Prime Minister Pierre Trudeau, the government had no business in citizens' bedrooms. In Poland, homosexuality was no longer considered a crime, though the decision only applied to homosexual prostitution. That same year, Daughters of Bilitis established an Australian branch in

Melbourne, which is generally regarded as Australia's first LGBT rights organization. In America, the Gay Liberation Front was established, making it the first LGBT group to include the word "gay" in its name. In West Germany, *Paragraph 175* was relaxed. Furthermore, the Cockettes debuted on December 31 at the Palace Theatre in San Francisco's North Beach district, located at Union and Columbus. "Satanism condones any type of sexual activity which properly satisfies your individual desires - be it heterosexual, homosexual, bisexual, or even asexual," wrote Anton Szandor LaVey in 1969 in regard to asexuals and asexuality in his book *The Satanic Bible.*

Campaign Against Moral Persecution, or CAMP, was established in Australia in **1970**. The Task Force on Gay Liberation, which is now known as the GLBT Round Table, was also established, making it the oldest LGBTQ-specific professional organization in the United States. New York City hosted the inaugural Gay Liberation Day March in the same year, and the first "Gay-in" was staged in San Francisco. Furthermore, *A Gay Manifesto* was penned by Carl Wittman, and after the arrest of a Young Liberals activist for importuning in November, the first gay rights march in the UK took place in Highbury Fields.

In September **1971**, Faygele Ben-Miriam and Paul Barwick petitioned for a marriage certificate in Seattle, Washington. This action sparked the 1974 lawsuit Singer v. Hara. Homosexuality was made legal in Austria, Costa Rica, and Finland, and the sodomy laws in Oregon and Colorado were repealed. Idaho's sodomy laws were also overturned before being reinstated as a result of objections from Mormons and Catholics. On February 6th, the Campaign Against Moral Persecution (CAMP) became a legal entity, and the first open meeting of homosexual men and women in Australia took place in a Balmain church hall. In Melbourne, Society Five was established. Furthermore, the first legally wed same-sex couple in American history was Richard John "Jack" Baker and James Michael McConnell, both of whom were born in 1942. They were "the first same-gender marriage ever to be documented in the official files of any civil government," according to another source. The sodomy prohibitions were among the victimless crime laws that were demanded to be repealed by the United States Libertarian Party, and Dr. Frank Kameny campaigned as the first openly homosexual candidate for Congress. The first collegiate LGBT programs office, formerly known as the "Gay Advocate's Office," was founded at the University of Michigan. The UK Gay Liberation Front (GLF) held weekly meetings with 200 to 300 attendees and was recognized as a political movement by the national press. The last person imprisoned for homosexual conduct in Canada, George Klippert, was released, and in Japan, Ken Togo ran for office. Betty Berzon made history by publicly declaring herself to be homosexual at a UCLA conference titled "The Homosexual in America." She was the first psychotherapist in the nation to do so. Furthermore, *Boys in the Sand*, which came out in 1969 and nearly a year before 1972's *Deep Throat*, was the first homosexual pornographic film to have credits, to be successful commercially and critically, and to be featured in *Variety*. It was also one of the first pornographic films to receive popular acceptance following Andy Warhol's 1969 *Blue Movie*. It had a New York City premiere, an advertising campaign unlike any other for a pornographic film, and it was an instant critical and financial triumph. Lastly, San Francisco saw the establishment of the first homosexual Democratic club in the country, the Alice B. Toklas

Democratic Club.

Nancy Wechsler, a member of the Human Rights Party was elected to the Ann Arbor City Council in **1972** and came out as a lesbian during her first and only time there, becoming the first openly homosexual or lesbian person to hold political office in America. *The Asexual Manifesto* was published in 1972 by Lisa Orlando on behalf of the New York Radical Feminists' Asexual Caucus. It defined an asexual as someone who "relates sexually to no one" and asexuality as a way of life that rejects sex unless it is "congruent with our values and totally incidental and unimportant to our relationships." The essay went on to list specific damaging beliefs about the value of sex in partnerships that are generally in line with the ideas of amatonormativity and compulsory sexuality. Hawaii officially legalized homosexuality, and homosexual activity was no longer a criminal offense in Norway. East Lansing, Michigan, Ann Arbor, Michigan, and San Francisco, California became the first cities in the United States to enact a homosexual rights ordinance. In South Australia, a legal defense was developed that catered to consenting adults in private, and Sweden became the first nation in the world to provide free hormone therapy and legal sex transition for transgender persons. The first openly gay and lesbian delegates to the Democratic Convention, Jim Foster of San Francisco and Madeline Davis of Buffalo, New York, presented the first statements in support of a homosexual rights plank in the Democratic Party Platform. Davis composed and performed *Stonewall Nation*, the first gay anthem, which was issued on a 45 rpm record by the Mattachine Society of the Niagara Frontier. Davis and Margaret Small instructed Lesbianism 101 at the University of Buffalo, which was the first lesbianism course offered in the country. Jeanne Manford, a schoolteacher from Queens, New York, participated in the Christopher Street Liberation Day march alongside her gay son Morty Manford, an activist for LGBT rights. Here was where the PFLAG (originally Parents of Gays, then Parents, Families and Friends of Lesbians and Gays, now simply PFLAG.) movement and the straight ally movement got their start. In the same year, while the judge imposed restrictions on the arrangement by forbidding Ms. Mitchell's lover from relocating in with her and the kids, Camille Mitchell made history by being the first open lesbian to be granted custody of her children in a divorce case. With the Metropolitan Community Church, Freda Smith became the organization's first openly lesbian preacher, who was also their first female minister. In addition to being the first LGBT synagogue recognized by the Union for Reform Judaism, Beth Chayim Chadashim was established in 1972. The *Ithaca Statement on Bisexuality* in favor of bisexuals was published by a Quaker organization called the Committee of Friends on Bisexuality. The declaration, which was published in the Quaker *Friends Journal* and *The Advocate*, was perhaps "the first public proclamation of the bisexual movement" and "was irrefutably the first statement on bisexuality made by an American religious assembly." Many Quaker organizations now hold different views on LGBT individuals and their rights, with some being more welcoming than others. Furthermore, Twin Peaks Tavern was the first homosexual pub in San Francisco to have clear windows after getting rid of its tinted ones, and the first book to look at homosexual Wicca and witchcraft was released by Jack Fritscher, titled *Popular Witchcraft Straight from the Witch's Mouth.*

Homosexuality was officially legalized in Malta in **1973**. Also, the Australian and New Zealand College of Psychiatry Federal Council, the first organization of its kind in the world to do so, declared that homosexuality was not a disease on October 15. In the United States, the American Psychiatric Association removed homosexuality from its *Diagnostic and Statistical Manual of Mental Disorders (DSM-II)*, largely as a result of Evelyn Hooker's research and advocacy. PFLAG held its first official meeting on March 26 at the Metropolitan-Duane Methodist Church in Greenwich Village (now the Church of the Village). The founder Jeanne Manford, her husband Jules, their son Morty, Dick and Amy Ashworth, Reverend Troy Perry, the founder of Metropolitan Community Church, and others were among the approximately 20 attendees. When Sally Miller Gearhart was hired by San Francisco State University that same year, she became the first open lesbian to be given a tenure-track professor post. She also assisted in founding one of the nation's first departments for women and gender studies. Furthermore, the first known album in the history of country music with a homosexual theme was released by the American country band Lavender Country. In order to endorse the concept of "picking your own label," activists at Barnard College were photographed and their picture appeared in the February/March 1973 issue of *Off Our Backs*. Asexuality was "an orientation that regards a partner as nonessential to sex, and sex as nonessential to a satisfying relationship," according to the article that inspired the distribution of the image.

The Community Softball League, which eventually had both men's and women's teams, was established in San Francisco as the first homosexual softball league in the world in **1974**. The teams, who were frequently supported by gay bars, played both against one another and the San Francisco Police softball team. Ohio's sodomy laws were repealed, and Dr. Fritz Klein established the first bisexual community support group, The Bisexual Forum, in New York City. In Los Angeles, the National Socialist League (The Gay Nazi Party) was established, and Chile became the second nation in the world to permit a trans person to legally change their name and gender on their birth certificate after undergoing sex reassignment surgery. Furthermore, Kathy Kozachenko was elected to the Ann Arbor, Michigan city council, making history as the first openly homosexual person to be elected to any political office in the United States. Also, the first openly LGBT telephone support line launched in London, and the Brighton Lesbian and Gay Switchboard followed a year later. When she won a seat in the Massachusetts State House, Elaine Noble became the second openly gay American elected to public office. Motivated by Noble, Minnesota state representative Allan Spear came out in a newspaper interview. The world's greatest collection of works by and about lesbians and their communities is housed in the Lesbian Herstory Archives, which opened to the public in the New York residence of lesbian couple Joan Nestle and Deborah Edel. With her nomination for *The Little Prince* under the category of Best Music, Original Song Score/Adaptation—which she shared with Alan Jay Lerner, Frederick Loewe, and Douglas Gamley—Angela Morley became the first openly transgender person to be nominated for an Academy Award. David Bowie, a musician and songwriter, talked about asexuality in an article titled "David Bowie in dialogue on sexuality with William S. Burroughs" in *Rolling Stone*.

After coming out in **1975**, Maureen Colquhoun was elected as the first openly lesbian MP in the UK. She was the first openly homosexual MP in the UK. The *Consenting Adult Sex Bill*, which Willie Brown created and successfully lobbied for in the state legislature, made homosexuality legal in California. For the first time in Australia, South Australia legalized homosexuality between consenting adults in a private setting, and Minneapolis became the first American city to enact civil rights protections for transgender people. The first gay American Indian liberation group, Gay American Indians, was established that same year, and by releasing one issue of the journal *Subarashi Onna* (Wonderful Women), twelve women became the first group of Japanese women to publicly identify as lesbians. The first openly gay American military member was Technical Sergeant Leonard Matlovich of the United States Air Force, who did so to protest their ban. Furthermore, the UK periodical *Gay Left* began publishing, and the first same-sex marriage licenses in the US were granted by a Boulder County, Colorado clerk Clela Rorex on March 26 to Dave McCord and Dave Zamora. She issued six permits, and six same-sex weddings took place as a consequence, but all of them were annulled later that year.

In **1976**, the Australian Capital Territory officially decriminalized homosexuality among consenting adults in a private setting in addition to equalizing the legal consent age. In Australia, both the Gay Teachers Group and the Homosexual Law Reform Coalition were established, and Japan saw the founding of the Association of Homosexual Liberation. Allan Spear, an openly gay state representative from Minnesota, won reelection. The first US Foreign Service officer to come out as gay was Tom Gallagher. As he wouldn't have been able to get a security clearance after that, he left the Foreign Service. Furthermore, *The Fancy Dancer*, Patricia Nell Warren's third book, was the first best-seller to include a homosexual priest and explore gay life in a small town. In the same year, a resolution affirming homosexuals as children of God who "have a full and equal claim upon the love, acceptance, and pastoral concern and care of the Church" was passed by the American Episcopal Church.

The first gay film festival took place in **1977** in San Francisco. That same year, Croatia, Montenegro, Slovenia, and Vojvodina officially decriminalized homosexuality. A Human Rights Ordinance was passed in Dade County, Florida, but it was overturned the following year as a result of a strident anti-homosexual rights campaign led by Anita Bryant. The prohibition of discrimination based on sexual orientation in the public and private sectors was first implemented in Quebec, making it the first jurisdiction larger than a city or county in the world to do so. Furthermore, in reaction to Boston police searching a residence outside of Boston, which outraged the LGBT community, the Boston-Boise Committee was established. The National Center for Lesbian Rights was established in the United States, while in Japan, both Front Runners and Platonica Club were established. Harvey Milk won the election for city-county supervisor in San Francisco, becoming the third openly homosexual man at the time of his election, the first openly gay or lesbian candidate to win a political position in the state of California, and the seventh openly gay or lesbian elected person nationwide. Jeffrey Weeks, a Welsh novelist, released *Coming Out*, and the LGBT pride flag's original eight-color design was unveiled. *Gaysweek*, the first prominent homosexual weekly magazine in New York City, released its inaugural issue, and the United Church of Christ appointed Anne Holmes as the first openly lesbian preacher. Moreover, serving the Diocese of New York, Ellen Barrett became the first openly lesbian priest to be ordained by the Episcopal Church in the United States. Also in that year, Mary F. Beal's *Angel Dance*, the country's first lesbian mystery novel, was released. In India, Shakuntala Devi published the first research on homosexuality. The ground-breaking coming-out documentary *Word Is Out: Stories of Some of Our Lives*, which was produced by Peter Adair, Nancy Adair, and the Mariposa Film Group, had its world premiere at the Castro Theater. The movie marked the debut of gay and lesbian filmmakers' first full-length documentary about LGBT identity. The first LGBT synagogue to have its own building was Beth Chayim Chadashim. On March 26, Frank Kameny and a dozen other representatives of the gay and lesbian community addressed Midge Costanza, the public liaison at the time, on the urgent need for changes to federal policy and legislation. They were led by the National Gay Task Force at the time. Gay rights were formally debated in the White House for the first time at this moment. One of the earliest scholarly works on asexuality was written by Myra Johnson and included in the book *The Sexually Oppressed*. She defined "asexuality" as the complete lack of sexual desire, and "autoerotic" individuals as those who did experience sexual desire but did not intend to satisfy it with others. Johnson concentrated on these women's issues because she believed that the feminist and sexual revolution movements of the period sometimes overlooked their issues.

The first known lesbian-feminist BDSM group, Samois, was established in San Francisco in **1978**. Patrick Califia and Gayle Rubin were prominent members of the organization, which is regarded as one of the very first proponents of sex-positive feminism. Also, the International Lesbian and Gay Association (ILGA) was founded. In the same year, 2000 persons attended the first Sydney Gay and Lesbian Mardi Gras; 53 of them were subsequently detained and several of them received violent beatings from law enforcement officers. The rainbow flag initially appeared as a representation of LGBT pride. During her appearance on a Phyllis Diller-hosted Showtime comedy special, Robin Tyler made history as the first out gay person to appear on American national television. She also published *Always a Bridesmaid, Never a Groom*, the first comedy album by an out lesbian, in the same year. Furthermore, Jon Reed Sims established the San Francisco Gay Freedom Day Marching Band and Twirling Corp. before renaming it the San Francisco Lesbian/Gay Freedom Band. It was the world's first openly homosexual musical ensemble when it was founded. With the submission of over 350 applications, San Francisco became the first city in America to hold a recruiting drive for homosexual police officers. Allen Bennett made history by becoming the country's first openly gay rabbi, and David Thorstad established the North American Man/Boy Love Association, a pedophile advocacy group that later joined the International Lesbian, Gay Association and had the backing of "the father of homosexual liberation," Harry Hay.

When Grady Quinn and Randy Rohl attended the Lincoln High School prom in Sioux Falls, South Dakota, on May 23, **1979**, they made history as the first known homosexual couple to attend a high school dance. In the same year, homosexuality was no longer a crime in Cuba and Spain, and Sweden was the first country to proclaim that homosexuality was no longer a disease. This happened as a result of some citizens of the nation reporting to work unwell with symptoms of "being homosexual" in opposition to homosexuality being labeled as a disease. The National Board of Health and Welfare's main office was then occupied by activists, and a few months later, Sweden removed homosexuality from its list of diseases. The Sisters of Perpetual Indulgence, who made their debut on Easter Sunday in San Francisco, and the Japan Gay Center were two LGBT organizations that were founded. The National March on Washington for Lesbian and Gay Rights, the first national march for gay rights, took place in Washington, D.C. The initial appeal for a Radical Faerie assembly in Arizona was made by Harry Hay. The Radical Faeries are an international network of loosely associated countercultural activists who seek to reinvent queer consciousness via secular spirituality. The movement, which is occasionally seen as a variation on contemporary paganism, also borrows ideas from anarchism and environmentalism. Furthermore, the first LGBT Hispanic bar in San Francisco, Esta Noche, opened its doors this year at 3079 16th & Mission Street. Also, Stephen Lachs was appointed as a judge for the first time in the history of the United States, and is regarded as the first openly homosexual judge ever appointed globally. Lastly, although Lesléa Newman's *Heather Has Two Mommies* occasionally receives this distinction in error, Jane Severance's picture book *When Megan Went Away*, written by Severance and illustrated by Tea Schook, was widely considered as the first picture book to contain LGBT characters, and especially the first to feature lesbian characters. Michael D. Storms reimagined the Kinsey Scale as a two-dimensional map that included asexuality, which was described as displaying little to no homo-eroticism or hetero-eroticism, in a research that was published in *Advances in the Study of Affect*. For the first time, asexuality was taken into consideration by this kind of scale. Storms hypothesized that a significant number of investigators using Kinsey's model would be mislabeling asexual people as bisexual because both were simply defined by not having a preference for one gender over another in a romantic relationship.

In **1980**, Scotland officially decriminalized homosexuality, and as the first homosexual rabbi in Britain, Lionel Blue made his sexual orientation public. In the same year, Steve Endean founded the Human Rights Campaign Fund, an organization that promotes LGBT causes. It was the largest civil rights organization in America working to advance LGBT equality. The Democratic Party of the United States became the first significant political party in the country to support a homosexual rights platform plank. From October 17 to 19, "Becoming Visible: The First Black Lesbian Conference" took place at the Women's Building. Since then, it has been recognized as the first conference for lesbian women of African descent. Furthermore, the Socialist Party of the United States nominated an openly homosexual man, David McReynolds, as its (and America's) first openly gay presidential candidate. The DSM-III, the first edition of the *DSM* to list a disease related to poor sexual desire, was released. In the 1987 edition of the DSM-III-R, this category—originally known as Inhibited Sexual Desire (ISD)—was separated into Hypoactive Sexual Desire Disorder (HSDD) and Sexual Aversion Disorder (SAD), the former pertaining to a lack of interest in sex and the latter to a phobic avoidance.

The US Centers for Disease Control and Prevention (CDC) released the first formal report on the condition that would be known as AIDS on June 5, **1981**. Homosexuality was no longer considered a criminal offense in Victoria and Columbia, both of which also enforced a uniform age of consent, and Norway became the first nation in the world to adopt a legislation prohibiting discrimination against homosexuals. The criminalization of homosexual conduct between consenting adults in Northern Ireland was invalidated by the European Court of Human Rights in the case of Dudgeon v. United Kingdom, which led to the nation's decriminalization of gay sex the following year. Furthermore, the first sex reassignment procedure in Hong Kong was performed. Also, when the relationship between tennis player Billie Jean King and her assistant Marilyn Barnett was made public in a May 1981 "palimony" lawsuit brought by Barnett, King became the first well-known professional athlete to come out as a lesbian. Her endorsements were all terminated as a result. With Jerry Brown's appointment of Mary C. Morgan to the San Francisco Municipal Court, she made history as the first openly homosexual or lesbian judge in the United States. The San Francisco Chronicle recruited Randy Shilts as a national correspondent, making him the first out homosexual reporter with a gay "beat" in the American mainstream press. Charles H. Cochrane Jr., a sergeant in the New York City Police Department, came out as homosexual before the city council. He became the first officer in the New York City Police Department to come out as gay. Lastly, the London Bisexual Group was established as the UK's first bisexual organization.

In **1982**, Portugal (for the second time) and Northern Ireland both decriminalized homosexuality, and Wisconsin was the first state in the United States to outlaw discrimination against homosexuals. Also, discrimination based on actual or perceived homosexuality was outlawed in New South Wales, making it the first state in Australia to do so, and Ken Togo established the Deracine Party in Japan. Furthermore, Sergeant Charles H. Cochrane Jr. of the New York City Police Department and Sam Ciccone, a retired sergeant from Fairview, New Jersey, founded the Gay Officers Action League (GOAL). It became the first organization that focused particularly on the requirements of LGBT law enforcement personnel. While the first openly gay mayor in American history was elected in Laguna Beach, Chris Dickerson won Mr. Olympia, making him the first out homosexual man to do so, and San Francisco hosted the first Gay Games, which drew 1,600 competitors.

In **1983**, Guernsey (including Alderney, Herm, and Sark) officially decriminalized homosexuality. Autumn Courtney, Lani Ka'ahumanu, Arlene Krantz, David Lourea, Bill Mack, Alan Rockway, and Maggi Rubenstein founded BiPOL in San Francisco, making it the nation's first and oldest bisexual political organization. Massachusetts Congressperson Gerry Studds came out as homosexual on the House floor, becoming the first openly gay member of Congress. Also, the first openly homosexual male municipal court judge in the State of California was appointed by Governor Jerry Brown to be Herb Donaldson. The Boston City Council elected David Scondras as its first openly homosexual representative, and Kitty Tsui published her debut book *Words of a Woman who Breathes Fire*, becoming the first known Asian American lesbian to do so. Furthermore, *Black Lesbian in White America*, written by Anita Cornwell, became the first published collection of writings by an African-American lesbian.

Paula Nurius' 1983 study on the connection between sexual orientation and mental health was the first to provide scientific information regarding asexuals. The research assessed participants based on their sexual behavior and desire using a variation of Kinsey's approach.

In **1984**, New South Wales and Australia's Northern Territory officially legalized homosexuality. The "Ten Percent Club" in Hong Kong, the Argentine Homosexual Community (Comunidad Homosexual Argentina, CHA), which brought together numerous distinct and pre-existing organisations, and ILGA Japan were all established. Gerry Studds was re-elected as a representative for Massachusetts by voters who were fully aware of his sexual orientation upon having come out the previous year. Chris Smith, a recent addition to the UK legislature, stated: "I go by Chris Smith. I'm gay and the Labour Party's representative for Islington South and Finsbury ", making him the first out gay male politician in the UK parliament (Maureen Colquhoun being the first openly out homosexual politician in the UK in 1975). The first American city to implement a program of domestic partnership health benefits for public employees was Berkeley, California. When West Hollywood was founded, it became the first city to elect a city council with a majority of openly homosexual or lesbian members. The first Jewish group to embrace openly homosexual and lesbian rabbis and cantors was Reconstructionist Judaism. Debi Sundahl and Myrna Elana published the first issue of *On Our Backs*, the country's first lesbian erotica publication for a lesbian audience, with contributions from Susie Bright, Nan Kinney, Honey Lee Cottrell, Dawn Lewis, Happy Hyder, Tee Corinne, Jewelle Gomez, Judith Stein, Joan Nestle, and Patrick Califia. Outside the Democratic National Convention in San

Francisco, the first bisexual rights demonstration was sponsored by BiPOL. Nine speakers from civil rights organizations associated with the bisexual movement spoke during the gathering.

In **1985**, France strictly enforced anti-discrimination laws that barred lifestyle discrimination in both employment and services. The Restoration Church of Jesus Christ (also known as the Gay Mormon Church) in Salt Lake City, Utah and the Bisexual Resource Center (BRC) in Massachusetts were founded, and in honor of LGBT Holocaust victims, the first memorial was established. AIDS took the life of actor Rock Hudson. He was the first well-known public figure to pass away from an AIDS-related disease, according to records. Terry Sweeney was "out" before being hired as a cast member, making him the first openly gay male cast member of *Saturday Night Live.* Furthermore, *Brookside*, a Liverpool-based soap opera, had the first openly homosexual character on British television.

In **1986**, the *Homosexual Law Reform Act*, which permitted sex between men over 16 lawful, legalized homosexuality in New Zealand. Haiti officially decriminalized homosexuality, while Ontario passed anti-discrimination legislation. The first openly lesbian couple in America to be approved for legal, joint adoption of a child were Becky Smith and Annie Afleck. From May 1 to May 3, Tokyo hosted the ILGA Asia Conference, and the Dutch Remonstrants were the first Christian group in the world to conduct same-sex unions and weddings. The role of Kate McBride, a police officer, was performed by Lindsay Crouse in *Hill Street Blues*, which introduced the first lesbian recurrent character on a major network.

In **1987**, the US government's tardy reaction to the AIDS pandemic led to the formation of the AIDS Coalition to

Unleash Power (ACT-UP). A group of bisexual New Yorkers, including Brenda Howard, founded the New York Area Bisexual Network (NYABN). The first referendum to outlaw discrimination based on sexual orientation was approved by citizens in Boulder, Colorado. Anti-discrimination legislation was enacted by the Canadian province of Manitoba and the Yukon territory. ACT UP organized its first significant protest, during which seventeen demonstrators were detained. Barney Frank, a member of the US Congress, came out and went on to become the country's first politician to voluntarily come out, and the Homomonument, a monument commemorating persecuted gays, opened in Amsterdam. In the Republic of Ireland, David Norris was the first openly homosexual person to be elected for public office that same year. Furthermore, 75 bisexuals participated in the first-ever national gathering of bisexuals, the March On Washington For Gay and Lesbian Rights. The *Civil Disobedience Handbook for the March* included an article by Lani Ka'ahumanu titled *"The Bisexual Movement: Are We Visible Yet?"*. It was the first piece on bisexuals and the newly formed bisexual movement to appear in a major lesbian or gay journal.

In **1988**, in terms of social services, taxes, and inheritances, Sweden was the first nation to establish legislation protecting homosexuals. Sodomy and male-to-male sex activities were no longer considered criminal acts in Belize and Israel (although the relevant section in the old British mandate law from 1936 was never enforced in Israel). Svend Robinson, a Canadian lawmaker, came out of the closet. David Norris appealed his case (Norris v. Ireland) to the European Court of Human Rights after losing cases in the Irish High Court and Irish Supreme

Court (in 1980 and 1983 respectively). The Irish statute that made male-to-male intercourse illegal was overturned by the European Court on the grounds of privacy, while homosexuality remained unlawful in Ireland until 1993. Reform Jewish congregation Shir Tikvah Congregation of Minneapolis' Stacy Offner became the first openly lesbian rabbi to be employed by a prominent Jewish community. Robert Dover made history by being the first out homosexual Olympic athlete.

In **1989**, Western Australia (although the age of consent was set at 21) and Liechtenstein officially decriminalized homosexuality. With the exception of the ability to adopt (until June 2010) and the right to be married in a church, Denmark was the first nation in the world to pass registered partnership legislation (similar to a civil union) for same-sex couples. Sally Jesse Raphael, the host of an American talk show, spoke with Toby (Jim Sinclair's alias), who at the time identified as androgynous and nonsexual. In the landmark case of Braschi v. Stahl Associates Co., the New York court ruled that a gay couple who had been cohabitating for ten years qualified as a family for the purposes of the Rent Control Regulations of New York City. According to the ruling in Miguel Braschi's favor, eviction protection "should not rest on fictitious legal distinctions or genetic history, but instead should find its foundation in the reality of family life."

In **1990**, the Australian state of Queensland and the UK Crown Dependency of Jersey officially decriminalized homosexuality. The Humsafar Trust (India) , OutRage! (UK), BiNet USA (USA), and Queer Nation (USA) were among the LGBT organizations that were established that same year. The World Health Organization made the statement that homosexuality was no longer an illness.

Football player Justin Fashanu was the first to speak out in the media as a professional, and the decision to accept openly homosexual and lesbian rabbis and cantors was made by Reform Judaism. Dale McCormick was the first open lesbian elected to a state Senate (she was elected to the Maine Senate). Lesbian and homosexual Jews were deemed to be full and equal members of the Jewish community by the Union for Reform Judaism in 1990. A report by their committee on homosexuality and rabbis was officially endorsed by the organization's main body, the Central Conference of American Rabbis (CCAR). They came to the conclusion that "all Jews are religiously equal regardless of their sexual orientation" and that "all rabbis, regardless of sexual orientation, be accorded the opportunity to fulfill the sacred vocation that they have chosen." The first National Bisexual Conference in America took place where it initially met under the name North American Multicultural Bisexual Network (NAMBN). This inaugural conference was sponsored by BiPOL and held in San Francisco in 1990. There were more than 450 attendees from 20 states and 5 foreign countries, and the mayor of San Francisco issued a proclamation designating June 23, 1990, as Bisexual Pride Day and praising the bisexual rights movement for its leadership in the fight of social justice.

In **1991**, homosexuality was no longer considered a criminal offense in the Bahamas, Hong Kong, and Ukraine. The red ribbon was initially utilized as a symbol of the HIV/AIDS campaign, and Canada's Nova Scotia introduced anti-discrimination legislation (sexual orientation). Sherry Harris became the first openly lesbian African-American elected official after being elected to the Seattle City Council in Washington. The first lesbian kiss on television took place between the fictitious C.J. Lamb (played by

Amanda Donohoe) and Abby (Michele Greene) on the show *L.A. Law*. In June 1991, the Chicago Gay and Lesbian Hall of Fame was established. The hall of fame is the first municipal institution of its kind in the United States, possibly the world.

In **1992**, homosexuality was no longer a crime in Estonia and Latvia, and Isle of Man, a UK Crown Dependency, officially abolished its sodomy laws (homosexuality was still illegal until 1994). Australia and Canada pushed for the lifting of a ban on gay individuals serving in the military, while Canadian provinces New Brunswick and British Columbia adopted anti-discrimination laws (sexual orientation). Serving a single term in the Massachusetts House of Representatives, Althea Garrison was elected as the nation's first transgender state representative; at the time of her election, her gender identity was not widely known. In New York City, Ana Mara Simo, Sarah Schulman, Maxine Wolfe, Anne-Christine d'Adesky, Marie Honan, and Anne Maguire founded the Lesbian Avengers. Japan hosted the Tokyo International Lesbian & Gay Film Festival, and *Assembly Bill 101*, which prohibited sexual orientation-based employment discrimination in California, was signed by Pete Wilson, the state's governor at the time. Futhermore, the first syndicated national column in the mainstream media to discuss homosexual life was written by Deb Price for The Detroit News in 1992.

In **1993**, Norway (without adoption until 2009, replaced with same-sex marriage in 2008/09) passed and implemented civil union or registered partnership legislation, and the Australian Territory of Norfolk Island officially repealed its sodomy legislation. Belarus, Ireland, Lithuania, the UK Crown Dependency of Gibraltar, and Russia (apart from the Chechen Republic) officially decriminalized homosexuality, and while Minnesota, a state in the United States addressed gender identity, Saskatchewan, a province in Canada protected sexual orientation as they adopted anti-discrimination laws. The *Human Rights Amendment Act*, passed by the New Zealand parliament, prohibited discrimination on the basis of sexual orientation or HIV, and they also lifted the ban on gay individuals serving in the military. Melissa Etheridge, an American singer, songwriter, musician, and guitarist revealed her sexual orientation, and the Triangle Ball, the country's first-ever inaugural gala honoring homosexuals and lesbians, was held. Twenty thousand women participated in the inaugural Dyke March, which was organized by the Lesbian Avengers for lesbians and their heterosexual female allies. Roberta Achtenberg was appointed by President Bill Clinton to the post of Assistant Secretary for Fair Housing and Equal Opportunity, making her the first openly homosexual or lesbian person to be nominated by the president and approved by the U.S. Senate. Lea DeLaria's performance on *The Arsenio Hall Show* made her the first openly homosexual comic to crack the late-night talk-show barrier. The first all-gay stand-up comedy special, *Out There* on Comedy Central, was presented by Lea DeLaria in December 1993. Esther D. Rothblum and Kathleen A. Brehony published *Boston Marriages: Romantic but Asexual Relationships Among Contemporary Lesbians*.

In **1994**, Israel passed and implemented a law recognizing unregistered cohabitation (without adoption, without step-adoption until 2005). South Africa passed anti-discrimination legislation (sexual orientation, interim constitution). Homosexuality was no longer considered a criminal offense in Bermuda, the UK Crown Dependency of Isle of Man, the Commonwealth of Australia, and Serbia. The American Medical Association asserted that homosexuality was no longer an illness. National Coalition for Gay and Lesbian Equality was established as an LGBT organization in South Africa. Homosexuals were granted refugee status by Canada because they feared for their wellbeing in their own country. Fear of being persecuted for their sexual orientation qualified individuals for asylum in the United States. Deborah Batts was appointed to the U.S. District Court in New York and became the first openly homosexual or lesbian federal judge. The United Nations Human Rights Committee (UNHRC) heard the historic human rights case of Toonen v. Australia in 1994 which was filed by Nicholas Toonen, a native of Tasmania. The case led to the abolition of Australia's last sodomy legislation when the Committee determined that sexual orientation was a protected status under the *International Covenant on Civil and Political Rights (ICCPR)* and was thus included in the anti-discrimination provisions. The Chinese New Year Parade in San Francisco included participation from the Gay Asian Pacific Alliance and Asian Pacific Sister, marking the first time LGBT Asian American communities had participated in a publicly ethnic event. Japan hosted the Gay Parade in August 1994. Wilson Cruz made history by being the first out homosexual actor to portray a major part in the television series *My So-Called Life*. One of the first publicly homosexual members of the U.S. Congress and the first openly gay U.S. Republican lawmaker, Steve Gunderson was outed as gay on the House floor by representative Bob Dornan (R-CA) during a discussion about government financing for LGBT-friendly curricula. The first pre-watershed lesbian kiss in the UK was shown on the soap opera *Brookside*, which is based in Liverpool. The commitment ceremony between Pedro Zamora and Sean Sasser, which was broadcasted on television in 1994 and included the couple exchanging vows, was regarded as a historic moment in the history of the medium. One in 100 people, according to Anthony Bogaert's research published in *The Journal of Sex Research*, classified as asexual.

In **1995**, laws governing civil unions and registered partnerships were passed and implemented in Sweden (with adoption, replaced with same-sex marriage in April 2009). Canadian province Newfoundland and Labrador introduced anti-discrimination statutes (sexual orientation). Homosexuality was no longer a crime in Moldova and Albania. HIV, the virus that causes AIDS, was demonstrated to be effectively treated by triple combination therapy using medications like 3TC, AZT, and ddC. Gay Advice Darlington/Durham was established by gay and bisexual men in the area and has grown into a charity that works with and for the LGBT community of County Durham and Darlington. The Human Rights Campaign expanded their mission to advocate for "an America where gay, lesbian, bisexual, and transgender people are ensured equality and embraced as full members of the American family at home, at work, and in every community" while dropping the word "Fund" from their name. In receiving an international Rhodes Scholarship, Rachel Maddow made history as the first openly homosexual or lesbian American to do so. The first homosexual rugby team in the world, Kings Cross Steelers, was established. *The Jewish Condition: Essays on Contemporary Judaism Honoring Rabbi Alexander M. Schindler* contained an essay by Rabbi Margaret Wenig titled "Truly Welcoming Lesbian and Gay Jews." It was the first Jewish publication to argue for homosexual couples' right to civil marriage. From 1993 until 2001, Ed Flanagan was the State Auditor of Vermont. In 1995, just before running for reelection in 1996, he came out as homosexual, making him the nation's first openly gay statewide-elected official.

In **1996**, Iceland passed and enacted civil union/registered partnership legislation (with step-adoption, without joint adoption until 2006, replaced with same-sex marriage in 2010). Hungary passed and implemented a law recognizing unregistered cohabitation (replaced with registered partnerships in 2009). Homosexuality was no longer considered a crime in North Macedonia, Macau, and Romania. Canada adopted anti-discrimination legislation (federal, sexual orientation). The fictitious characters Carol (played by Jane Sibbett) and Susan (played by Jessica Hecht) got married in the first lesbian wedding on television. In the same year, Californian Steve Fong, a member of the Log Cabin Republicans, became the first out homosexual speaker at a Republican National Convention. Muffin Spencer-Devlin became the first LPGA player to open up about her sexual orientation.

In **1997**, South Africa and Fiji introduced anti-discrimination legislation that addressed sexual orientation. Ecuador, Venezuela, and the Australian state of Tasmania officially decriminalized homosexuality. Similar to marriage, the UK granted same-sex couples immigration rights. One of the first famous people to come out as a lesbian was Ellen DeGeneres. Moreover, later that year Ellen DeGeneres became the first out lesbian actress to play an openly lesbian character on television when her character Ellen Morgan came out as a lesbian on the television program *Ellen*. Patria Jiménez, who ran for the

Party of the Democratic Revolution, became the first openly homosexual person to win a seat in the Mexican Congress. The first peer-reviewed, multidisciplinary publication devoted to LGBT health was published by the Gay and Lesbian Medical Association and was titled the *Journal of the Gay and Lesbian Medical Association*. On ABC's *Relativity*, the first open-mouth kiss between two women appeared on prime-time television. The article *Personal Definitions of Sexuality* by activist Jim Sinclair, which was initially written as a response to a class project in 1987, was released on their website. In it, Sinclair classified themselves as asexual. *My existence as an amoeba* by Zoe O'Reilly, a first-person examination of asexuality that triggered reactions throughout the late 1990s and early 2000s from those who connected with it, was published in the *StarNet Dispatches* webzine.

In **1998**, laws governing civil unions and registered partnerships were passed and put into force in the Spanish autonomous community of Catalonia. Legal protections against discrimination included those in the constitutions of Ecuador (sexual orientation), Ireland (sexual orientation), and the Canadian provinces of Alberta (court ruling only; legislation amended in 2009) and Prince Edward Island (sexual orientation). Bosnia and Herzegovina, the Republic of Cyprus, Kazakhstan, Kyrgyzstan, South Africa (retroactive to 1994), and Tajikistan were among the countries that decriminalized homosexuality. The ban on gay people serving in the military was lifted in Romania and South Africa. After a vote at their annual meeting in San Francisco, Parents and Friends of Lesbians and Gays added gender identity to their mission statement. For its efforts, Parents and Friends of Lesbians and Gays became the first national LGBT group to formally adopt a transgender-inclusion policy. Tammy Baldwin defeated Josephine Musser to win Wisconsin's 2nd congressional district seat, making history as the first openly gay or lesbian non-incumbent and the first open lesbian ever elected to Congress. With the song *Diva*, Dana International of Israel became the first transgender person to win the Eurovision Song Contest. Robert Halford comes out of the closet and becomes his genre's first openly homosexual musician. On December 5, 1998, the first bisexual pride flag was displayed. On *Coronation Street*, Julie Hesmondhalgh portrayed Hayley Anne Patterson, the first transgender character on British television. BiNet USA served as the host for the First National Institute on Bisexuality and HIV/AIDS.

In **1999**, the US State of California passed and implemented civil union/registered partnership legislation (without adoption, without step adoption until 2001, same-sex marriage in June 2008 – November 2008). Chile officially decriminalized homosexuality. "Queer Youth Alliance," an LGBT organization, was founded in the UK. In South Africa, same-sex partners were eligible for spousal immigration benefits. France passed and implemented civil union/registered partnership legislation. Israel's top court recognized a lesbian partner as a second legal mother of her partner's biological son. In an article for the Israeli daily *Maariv*, Steven Greenberg officially admitted to being homosexual. He was generally referred to as the first out gay Orthodox Jewish rabbi because he received his ordination at the Yeshiva University's Orthodox rabbinical seminary (RIETS). Yet, many rabbis and some Orthodox Jews disputed his status as an Orthodox rabbi. Gwendolyn Ann Smith, a trans woman who worked as a graphic designer, columnist, and activist, established the

Transgender Day of Remembrance in 1999 to honor Rita Hester's murder in Allston, Massachusetts. TDoR was launched by Smith as a web-based project, and every year on November 20 since then, it has become an annual international day of action. Michael Page, Gigi Raven Wilbur, and Wendy Curry organized the inaugural Celebrate Bisexuality Day in the same year.

In the year **2000**, the State of Vermont in the United States passed and implemented civil union/registered partnership legislation. South Africa introduced anti-discrimination legislation (hate speech, harassment). Discriminatory laws (*Section 28*) were repealed in the UK subdivision of Scotland. The United Kingdom lifted the ban on gay persons serving in the military. Georgia and Azerbaijan officially decriminalized homosexuality. In Germany, the Bundestag formally expressed remorse for the harm done to homosexual individuals up to 1969 as well as for the persecution of homosexuals and lesbians during the Nazi era. For immigration reasons, Israel recognized same-sex relationships between an Israeli resident and their foreign partner. At a pride parade in Phoenix, Arizona, the transgender pride flag was first flown. In an LGBT pride parade, Hillary Clinton made history as the first First Lady to march. Jim Kolbe made history by being the first openly homosexual speaker at the Republican National Convention, albeit he avoided discussing gay rights in his remarks.

In **2001**, in the Netherlands, joint adoption brought about the implementation of same-sex marriage regulations. In Germany, civil union/registered partnership legislation was implemented without adoption until October 2004 and then only with step-adoption. In Finland, regulations governing civil unions and registered partnerships were approved without step-adoption until May 2009. Without joint adoption, Portugal approved and implemented limited partnership regulations (replaced with marriage in 2010). The Swiss canton of Geneva passed limited partnership regulations without a joint adoption. Maryland and Rhode Island, two US states, passed anti-discrimination laws that apply to the private sector and sexual orientation. The sodomy laws in the US state of Arizona were abolished. The remaining regions of the United Kingdom decriminalized homosexuality. In China, homosexuality was deemed to no longer be an illness. In Desert Memorial Park in Cathedral City, California, the nation's first monument honoring LGBT veterans was officially unveiled. The Netherlands' Helene Faasen and Anne-Marie Such became the first two women to officially marry. The first permanent, free-standing memorial in America to the tens of thousands of gays who were persecuted by Nazi Germany during the Holocaust was unveiled as Pink Triangle Park. The Asexual Visibility and Education Network (AVEN), formed by David Jay in 2001, grew to be the largest and best-known of the several asexual groups that have emerged since the emergence of the World Wide Web and social media.

In **2002**, the Canadian province of Quebec passed and brought civil union/registered partnership laws into effect with joint adoption. Finland's civil union/registered partnership laws came into effect without joint adoption until May 2009, then with step-adoption. The Argentinian city of Buenos Aires passed civil union/registered partnership laws without joint adoption. The Swiss canton of Zurich passed limited partnership laws without joint adoption. South Africa and Sweden legalized same-sex couple adoption with joint and step adoption.

Discrimination on the basis of sexual orientation was prohibited in the public and private sectors in the US states of Alaska and New York respectively. This was achieved by passing anti-discrimination legislation in these states. The Northwest Territories of Canada became the first region in the country to outlaw discrimination based on gender identity, and all other Canadian provinces and territories would follow suit by 2017. The sodomy statutes of Romania, Costa Rica, Arkansas, and Massachusetts were repealed. Transgender Network, widely known as TNET, was founded by Parents and Friends of Lesbians and Gays as its first official "Special Affiliate," recognized with the same rights and obligations as its regular chapters. The Reform rabbi Margaret Wenig conducted the first school-wide course at any rabbinical school that addressed the psychological, legal, and theological difficulties impacting persons who are intersex or transsexual at the Reform seminary Hebrew Union College-Jewish Institute of Religion in New York. The *Sexual Orientation Non-Discrimination Act*, which was approved by New York in 2002, was the only legal document in existence at the moment to make reference to asexuality.

In **2003**, Belgium passed and brought same-sex marriage laws into effect (without joint adoption until Apr 2006). Civil union/registered partnership laws were passed in the Australian state of Tasmania (step adoption only). The Canadian provinces of Ontario and British Columbia passed and brought same-sex marriage laws into effect. Civil union/registered partnership laws came into effect in the Argentinian city of Buenos Aires (without joint adoption). Limited Partnerships laws came into effect in Austria without joint adoption, and was replaced with registered partnerships in 2010. Limited Partnerships laws came into effect in Croatia without registration or adoption. Discrimination on the basis of sexual orientation was outlawed in all sectors of Bulgaria and the United Kingdom (excluding religious organisations). Discrimination on the basis of sexual orientation was outlawed in the public sector of the US state of Arizona, while in Kentucky discrimination on the basis of sexual orientation and gender identity was prohibited. In the executive branch of the state government of Michigan, discrimination on the basis of sexual orientation was disallowed. New Mexico's private sector was prohibited from discrimination on the basis of sexual orientation and gender identity. Discrimination on the basis of gender identity in the public sector of Pennsylvania was outlawed. An end to ban on gay people in the military was sanctioned in Russia. Armenia repealed its sodomy laws, and the United Kingdom repealed the concept of Buggery in law. Iraq, Armenia and United States decriminalized homosexuality, and *Section 28* was repealed in England and Wales and Northern Ireland. Gene Robinson was elected as the first openly homosexual bishop of the American Episcopal Church. Reuben Zellman was ordained in 2010 and was the first openly transgender person to be approved by the Hebrew Union College-Jewish Institute of Religion. The Committee on Jewish Law and Standards approved a rabbinic opinion in 2003 that said sex reassignment surgery (SRS) was permissible as a therapy for gender dysphoria and that SRS changes a transgender person's sex status in accordance with Jewish law. In Australia, Alex MacFarlane was known to be the first person to acquire a birth certificate and passport with an unspecified gender. The Reconstructionist Rabbinical College's first campus-wide seminar on the psychological, judicial, and theological challenges impacting intersex or transgender persons was arranged in 2003 by Reform rabbi Margaret Wenig. The first bestseller written by an openly transgender American was Jennifer Finney Boylan's autobiography, *She's Not There: A Life in Two Genders*. Although not a sexual scene, *Buffy the Vampire Slayer* had girlfriends Tara Maclay and Willow Rosenberg in bed together in what was thought to be a first for a televised network series. Patrick Harvie became the first openly bisexual Lawmaker in Scotland.

In **2004**, legislation legalizing same-sex marriages was introduced in the Canadian provinces of Manitoba, Newfoundland and Labrador, Nova Scotia, Quebec, and Saskatchewan, the Canadian territory of Yukon, and the US State of Massachusetts. Civil union/registered partnership laws were passed and came into effect in the Brazilian state of Rio Grande do Sul, Luxembourg, and the US state of Maine. They also came into effect in the Australian state of Tasmania and were just passed in New Zealand. Limited partnership laws were passed and came into effect in New Jersey. Adoption for same-sex couples was legalized in Germany. Anti-discrimination legislation was introduced in Portugal, and in the US states of Indiana, Louisiana, and Maine. Cape Verde, Marshall Islands, and San Marino saw the decriminalization of homosexuality. *The L Word* featured the first all-lesbian ensemble cast on television. The *Vagina Monologues* were performed for the first time exclusively by trans people. Eighteen prominent transgender women performed the monologues, and a new monologue on the hardships and experiences of transgender women was also included. When San Francisco mayor Gavin Newsom permitted city hall to issue marriage licenses to same-sex couples, Del Martin and Phyllis Lyon became the first same-sex couple to be wed in the country. All same-sex unions, however, were declared null and void in California in 2004. *Asexuality: prevalence and associated factors in a national probability sample* was published in 2004 in the *Journal of Sex Research* by psychologist Anthony F. Bogaert. This study found that 1% of a British probability sample from 1994 reported having no attraction to either men or women. In reaction to Bogaert's work, *The New Scientist* published an article on asexuality. *The Sex Files* on Discovery devoted an entire show on asexuality. Del Martin and Phyllis Lyon remarried and became the first same-sex couple in the state to wed following the 2008 California Supreme Court ruling that gave same-sex couples in the state the legal right to wed. Nonetheless, weddings that took place between the California Supreme Court ruling recognizing same-sex unions and the passage of *Prop* 8 were still regarded as lawful, including the union of Del Martin and Phyllis Lyon, which took place later in 2008 when *Prop* 8 outlawed same-sex unions in California. Then-New Jersey Governor James McGreevey came out as homosexual, making him the first openly gay state governor in US history. Soon after, he submitted his resignation. Bisi Alimi was the first Nigerian to publicly announce his homosexuality. *Luna*, written by Julie Anne Peters, was the first young-adult book containing a transgender character to be issued by a major publisher. In San Francisco in 2004, the first Transgender pride march took place. In 2004, Karamo Brown began his career in television as the first openly homosexual black guy on reality TV's *The Real World: Philadelphia* on MTV.

In **2005**, same-sex marriage laws were passed in Canada (nationwide) and Spain (with joint adoption). Civil union/registered partnership laws were passed in Andorra, United Kingdom (without joint adoption (in England and Wales until December 2005, without joint adoption in Scotland until Sep 2009, and without joint adoption in Northern Ireland), the US state of Connecticut, New Zealand (without joint adoption), US state of California, Switzerland (without adoption) and Slovenia. In the same year, same-sex couple adoption legalisation was introduced in the UK Subdivisions of England and Wales. Puerto Rico repealed its sodomy laws. The Parti Québécois elected André Boisclair as its leader, making him the first openly homosexual man to hold that position in North America. East-Central Minnesota Pride, the first rural LGBT pride in North America, was hosted in Pine City, Minnesota. For the first time, a whole episode of a cartoon series—*The Simpsons*—was devoted to the subject of same-sex unions. The inaugural meeting of the European Transgender Council took place in Vienna. The Human Rights Commission of the City and County of San Francisco released its first human rights report on the plight of intersex individuals. Eli Cohen was appointed a rabbi by the Jewish Renewal Movement, being the first openly gay man to do so. The first American male team-sport professional athlete who was publicly homosexual while playing was Andrew Goldstein. His local Major League Lacrosse team, the Boston Cannons, selected him in the 2005 draft after he officially came out in 2003. From 2005 to 2007, Goldstein played goalie with the Long Island Lizards, starting two games in 2006. A black ring placed on the right middle finger was a common symbol of the asexual community. It didn't matter what the ring was made of or how it had been made as long as it was mostly black. In 2005, this symbol first appeared on AVEN. Stephen Hillenburg disclosed SpongeBob SquarePants' asexuality.

In **2006**, South Africa (with joint adoption) passed same-sex marriage laws, while civil union/registered partnership laws were passed by the Czech Republic (without joint adoption), Slovenia, Mexico City, and the US state of New Jersey. Limited partnership laws were passed by the Australian State of South Australia, and abroad unions were recognized in Israel. Croatia's Zagreb hosted the first regional celebration of Eastern European pride. Springfield, Missouri, removed its ban on gay solicitation. Montreal hosted the World Conference on LGBT Human Rights. In Yogyakarta, Indonesia, the original *Yogyakarta Principles* were adopted. In the Isle of Man, Section 28 was successfully abolished. The first openly lesbian rabbis to be ordained by the Jewish Renewal movement were Chaya Gusfield and Rabbi Lori Klein, both of whom received their ordinations in America. Lesbian rabbis and cantors were now accepted in conservative Judaism. Elliot Kukla was the first openly transgender person to be ordained by the Hebrew Union College-Jewish Institute of Religion. He came out as transgender six months prior to his ordination in 2006. When she was elected in 2006, state representative Patricia Todd, a Democrat from Birmingham, became the state's first openly homosexual public servant. The first transgender person to be elected to statewide office in Hawaii was Kim Coco Iwamoto. In the Republic of Ireland, Bernard Lynch became the first Catholic priest in history to enter into a civil partnership (he had previously had his relationship blessed in a ceremony in 1998 by an American Cistercian monk). After being dismissed from his religious organization in 2011, he married his husband in a ceremony that was legally recognized in 2016. David Jay made appearances on *The View* on ABC in January 2006 and Tucker Carlson's *Tucker* show on MSNBC in March of the same year. He spoke about asexuality on both shows.

In **2007**, same-sex marriage laws were passed in Aruba, Curaçao, and Sint Maarten (Recognition of Dutch same-sex marriages only). Civil union/registered partnership laws were passed in the Mexican state of Coahuila, Mexico City, Switzerland (without adoption), the US state of New Jersey, Hungary (with adoption), the US state of New Hampshire, and Uruguay (without adoption until Sep 2008). Limited partnership laws were passed in the US states of Washington and Colombia, the Australian state of South Australia and the US state of Oregon. Istanbul, Turkey hosted the very first LGBT pride march to ever take place in a Muslim nation. The first presidential forum in the US to expressly address LGBT problems was held on the Logo cable channel. There were six Democratic Party candidates present. Republican candidates were asked to attend but declined. In the ABC drama *Dirty Sexy Money*, Candis Cayne portrayed Carmelita Rainer, a transsexual woman having an affair with married New York Attorney General Patrick Darling (played by William Baldwin). As the first openly transgender actress to play a recurring transgender character in prime time, Cayne made history with the part. The first overseas homosexual wedding took place on November 29 in Hanoi, Vietnam, between a Japanese and an Irish citizen. The Vietnamese gay and lesbian community paid close attention to the wedding. The first openly lesbian cantor ordained by the Jewish Renewal movement was a German woman named Jalda Rebling, who was born in the Netherlands. When Rabbi Toba Spitzer was chosen president of the Reconstructionist Rabbinical Assembly during the organization's annual conference in Scottsdale, Arizona, she made history by becoming the first openly lesbian or LGBT person to lead a rabbinical assembly. Joy Ladin was hired as an Orthodox university's first openly transgender lecturer (Stern College for Women of Yeshiva University). For México Posible, Amaranta Gómez Regalado made history by being the first transgender person to address the Mexican Congress. The first open lesbian to present at the Academy Awards was Ellen DeGeneres. The first street in California to be formally dedicated to a known lesbian was Ventura Place in Studio City, which was renamed Dr. Betty Berzon Place in her honor. Theresa Sparks became the first openly transgender person to be elected president of any San Francisco body and the city's highest-ranking openly transgender official when she was chosen by a single vote to lead the San Francisco Police Commission.

In **2008**, same-sex marriage laws were passed in Norway (with joint adoption), and the US states of California (May–Nov 2008), Connecticut, Florida and Mashantucket Pequot. Civil union/registered partnership laws were passed in the Australian Capital Territory, Ecuador (without joint adoption), the US states of Washington (expansion of previous legislation), New Hampshire, and Uruguay (without joint adoption until Sep 2008). Limited partnership laws were passed in the Australian state of Victoria and the US state of Oregon. Same-sex couple adoption legalisation was enacted in Uruguay. Nicaragua and Panama decriminalized homosexuality. The first ever gay Pride took place in Bulgaria. The first out homosexual athlete to win an Olympic gold medal was Matthew Mitcham. The first of its type in Eastern Europe, Kosovo declared its independence and enacted a new constitution that mentioned "sexual orientation." On the Greek island of Tilos, the first two same-sex civil weddings (two men and two women) were conducted. The chief prosecutor of the supreme court and the minister of justice declared the unions null and illegal. Sam Adams became the first out homosexual mayor of a top-30 U.S. city when he was chosen to lead Portland, Oregon. The first openly homosexual or lesbian mayor of Houston, TX, is Annise Parker. In the 2008 elections, Kate Brown won the position of Oregon Secretary of State, making history as the country's first openly bisexual statewide official. As the first openly transgender mayor in America, Stu Rasmussen was elected in Silverton, Oregon. The House Subcommittee on Health, Employment, Labor, and Pensions held the first-ever hearing in the history of the United States Congress on discrimination against transgender persons in the workplace. When Rachel Maddow started presenting *The Rachel Maddow Show* on American cable network MSNBC, she made history by being the first openly homosexual or lesbian anchor of a significant prime-time news program in the United States. The first openly lesbian United States Poet Laureate was Kay Ryan.

In **2009**, same-sex marriages laws were passed in Sweden (with joint adoption), the US states of Iowa, New Hampshire (step adoption only), Maine, WashingtonD.C. and Vermont, Norway (with joint adoption), the Coquille Indian Tribe, and Mexico City (with joint adoption). Civil union/registered partnership laws were enacted in Hungary (without joint adoption), Colombia (expansion of previous rights without joint adoption), Austria (without joint adoption), and the US states of Nevada and Washington (expansion of previous rights). Limited partnership laws were passed in the US states of Colorado and Wisconsin. Same-sex couple adoption legalisation was introduced in Finland (step adoption) and the UK Subdivision of Scotland. Argentina, Philippines and

Uruguay lifted their ban on LGBTQIA+ individuals serving in the miliitary.In 2009, transgender activist Rachel Crandall of Michigan established the International Transgender Day of Visibility in response to the dearth of LGBT holidays honoring transgender people. She expressed her frustration that the only recognized transgender holiday was the Transgender Day of Remembrance, which honored the lives lost to hate crimes but did not recognize and celebrate transgender people who were still alive. Jóhanna Sigurðardóttir, the first openly homosexual head of state ever elected, represented Iceland. With Annise Parker's election as mayor of Houston, Texas, the country's biggest city had an openly homosexual mayor. Diego Sanchez was employed as a legislative assistant for Barney Frank, making him the first openly transgender person to serve on Capitol Hill. In 2008, Sanchez was also the first transgender person to serve on the Platform Committee of the Democratic National Committee (DNC). The Democratic National Committee's first openly transgender member, Barbra "Babs" Siperstein, was nominated and elected as an at-large member. The adoption rights of Uzi Even and his life partner were the first to be officially recognized in Israel among same-sex male couples. Gareth Thomas, a Welsh rugby player, made history as the first top-tier professional male athlete in a team sport to come out while still competing. The first openly lesbian or homosexual Poet Laureate of the United Kingdom was Carol Ann Duffy. Kitzen and Jeni Branting exchanged vows at the Coos Bay plankhouse, a three-year-old gathering place constructed in the traditional Coquille manner with cedar plank walls. The tribe, of which Kitzen was a member, officially acknowledged their marriage for the first time as a same-sex couple. The San Francisco Pride

Celebration Committee chose LGBT activist Amy Andre as executive director in October 2009, making her the organization's first openly bisexual woman of color. The first Israeli orthodox rabbi to come out was Ron Yosef, who appeared in an episode of Israel's top investigative television program *Uvda* (Fact) in 2009 that discussed conversion therapy in that country. Yosef continued to serve as a pulpit Rabbi. The first comprehensive prayer book that addressed the needs and lifestyles of LGBTQ people as well as heterosexual Jews, *Siddur Sha'ar Zahav*, was released. As they marched in the San Francisco Pride Parade in 2009, AVEN members took part in the first asexual entry at an American pride parade.

In **2010**, same-sex marriage laws were passed in Portugal (without joint adoption), Iceland (with joint adoption), Argentina (with adoption), Mexico City (with joint adoption), and the US states of New Hampshire (step adoption only) and Washington D.C. No additional jurisdiction was necessary to execute marriages that were entered into in Mexico City, according to the Supreme Court of Mexico. The Australian state of Tasmania recognized same-sex marriages that took place in other countries. California's Proposition 8 was declared unconstitutional by United States District Judge Vaughn Walker as a breach of the Equal Protection and Due Process Clauses of the Fourteenth Amendment to the United States Constitution. Civil union/registered partnership laws were passed in Austria (without adoption and IVF access rights) and Ireland (without adoption rights). Limited partnership laws were enacted in the Australian state of New South Wales (without joint adoption until Sep 2010). Same-sex couple adoption legislation was introduced in Denmark and the Australian state of New South Wales. Homosexuality was no longer a criminal offense in Fiji. St. Petersburg hosted Russia's first-ever official LGBT pride march. Thomas Beatie, a transgender man, was named the "First Married Man to Give Birth" in the world by the Guinness World Records. When Amanda Simpson was hired as a senior technical adviser in the Bureau of Industry and Security of the Commerce Department, she made history as the nation's first openly transgender presidential appointment. As the first openly transgender basketball player in the NCAA, Kye Allums made history. He participated on the women's team at George Washington University as a transgender guy. The first openly transgender judge to be appointed in the US was Phyllis Frye. Mary Albing served the Lutheran Church of Christ the Redeemer on the south side of Minneapolis as the first openly lesbian minister to be ordained by the Evangelical Lutheran Church in America. Lesbian Chai Feldblum was the first openly LGBT person to hold a position at the Equal Employment Opportunity Commission (EEOC). Donna Ryu was appointed as a judge of the United States District Court, Northern District of California, becoming the first Asian-American woman, first Korean-American, and first lesbian to hold the position. Being the first openly transgender man, the first wheelchair user, and the first representative of New Mexico to win International Mr. Leather, Tyler McCormick made history. 2010 saw the public debut of the asexual pride flag. The four horizontal stripes on the asexual pride flag are, from top to bottom, black, grey, white, and purple. Sara Beth Brooks established Asexual Awareness Week, or Ace Week, in 2010. It takes place in the second part of October and was designed to raise awareness and celebrate asexual, aromantic, demisexual, and grey-asexual pride.

In **2011**, same-sex marriage laws were passed in New York and the Suquamish Tribe. Civil union/registered partnership laws were enacted in Ireland (without adoption rights), Isle of Man (with joint adoption), Liechtenstein, and the US states of Illinois (with joint adoption rights), Rhode Island, Delaware (came into effect in 2013) and Hawaii (came into effect Jan 2012). The United States of America lifted the ban on LGBTQIA+ people serving in the military via the *Don't Ask, Don't Tell* policy. Towards the end of November, Tony Briffa, who is thought to be the first intersex mayor in history, was elected in the Melbourne, Australia, suburb of Hobsons Bay. On December 6, Elio Di Rupo was appointed Prime Minister of Belgium and became the country's first openly homosexual person in office. In 2011, Chaz Bono participated in the 13th season of *Dancing with the Stars* in the US. This was the first time, a man who is openly transgender appeared on a major network television show for a role unrelated to his gender identity. When Harmony Santana was nominated by the Independent Spirit Awards for Best Supporting Actress in the film *Gun Hill Road*, she made history as the first openly transgender actress to get a significant acting award nomination. The ordination of openly homosexual and lesbian clergy was approved by the Presbyterian Church (USA). By receiving her ordination from the Jewish Theological Seminary of the Conservative faith, Rachel Isaacs became the first openly lesbian rabbi. Brenda Sue Fulton became the first openly LGBT member of the advisory board for the Academy after being appointed to the West Point Board of Visitors. Claire Buffie, Miss New York, made history as the first Miss America candidate to run for the crown on a platform supporting lesbian rights. When Jaiyah "Johnny" Saelua played for American Samoa in the opening round of Oceania's World Cup qualifiers for Brazil in 2014, she made history as the first openly transgender athlete to compete in the World Cup. On June 17, 2011, the UN Human Rights Council approved a resolution by South Africa (A/HRC/17/L.9/Rev.1) that called for research on prejudice and sexual orientation. This was the first time a resolution endorsing the rights of LGBT persons had been accepted by a United Nations body. America's first out homosexual Republican presidential candidate, Fred Karger launched his unsuccessful run for the 2012 GOP presidential nomination. *Bisexual Invisibility: Impacts and Regulations*, a report on bisexual visibility published by San Francisco's Human Rights Commission, was the first time a governmental entity had done so. As the first openly LGBT African-American to be accepted into the Reconstructionist Rabbinical College, Sandra Lawson made history.

In **2012**, same-sex marriage laws were passed in Denmark, the Mexican state of Quintana Roo, the U.S. states of Maine, Maryland and Washington, and the Port Gamble S'Klallam Tribe. Civil union/registered partnership laws were enacted in the U.S. state of Hawaii. Lesotho and São Tomé and Príncipe decriminalized homosexuality. Anti-discrimination legislation was introduced in Chile to battle discrimination based on sexual orientation and gender identity. A rule banning discrimination against LGBT people in federally supported housing programs was released by the Office of Fair Housing and Equal Opportunity of the U.S. Department of Housing and Urban Development. The new rules made sure that all qualified individuals, regardless of sexual orientation or gender identity, could participate in the Department's key housing programs. For discrimination on the basis of gender identity and gender expression respectively, the Canadian provinces of Manitoba and Ontario introduced anti-discrimination legislation. A divorce was granted by an Israeli family court to the country's first homosexual couple. According to *Haaretz*, the Ramat Gan Family Court approved Avi Even's divorce from Amit Kama, the first openly homosexual Knesset member. The court also instructed the Interior Minister to record their divorce. Avi Even was a professor at Tel Aviv University. Fish Huang and You Ya-ting got married in Taiwan's first same-sex Buddhist ceremony, with Buddhist master Shih Chao-hui officiating the ceremony. A young lieutenant and her partner (Ellen Schick and Shannon Simpson) were married for the first time at the U.S. Military Academy in the Old Cadet Chapel in West Point's graveyard. On a U.S. military base, Navy Chief Elny McKinney and Anacelly McKinney were married, making history as the first known same-sex union. They exchanged vows at San Diego's Naval Station Point Loma. The White House saw the first same-sex engagement (Ben Schock and Matthew Phelps). Air Force Col. Ginger Wallace was the first openly gay person in the U.S. military to invite their same-sex partner to the pinning ceremony, which had previously been limited to spouses and close relatives. Days after the two of them attended President Obama's State of the Union address as the First Lady's guests, Wallace was given colonel wings by her longtime companion of ten years, Kathy Knopf. The first openly lesbian cast member of *Saturday Night Live* was Kate McKinnon. Danitra Vance never came out in public but was identified as a lesbian after her passing. Diana King came out as a lesbian to her fans on June 28, 2012, on her official Facebook page, making history as the first Jamaican performer to do so. The first out lesbian to be ordained by the Presbyterian Church was Katie Ricks (USA). The first publicly transgender female rabbi was Emily Aviva Kapor, an American who was privately ordained by a "Conservadox" rabbi in 2005 and started living as a woman in 2012. A project called *Rainbow Jews* was launched to document the lives of Jewish bisexual, lesbian, gay, and transgender persons in the UK from the 1950s to the present. It is the first repository of Jewish bisexual, lesbian, gay, and transgender history in the United Kingdom. The first openly gay character in a popular animated film was in *ParaNorman*, which was released in 2012. On May 9, Barack Obama became the first US president to formally declare his support for same-sex marriages. Marlene Pray was the first openly bisexual public official in Pennsylvania when she joined the Doylestown, Pennsylvania City Council in 2012 and resigned in 2013. The first openly lesbian or homosexual U.S. senator was Tammy Baldwin. The first openly bisexual politician elected to the US Congress is Kyrsten Sinema (D-AZ). In Wisconsin's 2nd Congressional District, Mark Pocan won the election, becoming the first openly homosexual politician to succeed an openly gay member of Congress (in this case Tammy Baldwin). The first openly homosexual candidate to win a seat in Congress for New York was Sean Patrick Maloney. Mark Takano became the first openly homosexual person of color to be elected to the U.S. Congress. He was chosen to represent the 41st Congressional District of California. Josh Boschee became the first openly homosexual lawmaker in North Dakota after winning the election. As the first openly homosexual state representative in West Virginia, Stephen Skinner was elected. The first openly homosexual man to serve as a state representative in New Mexico was Jacob Candelaria. When he was elected, Brian Sims became the state's first openly homosexual lawmaker in Pennsylvania. The first out homosexual state politician in Pennsylvania was Rep. Mike Fleck, who came out after Brian Sims was elected but before he assumed office. As the first openly homosexual state representative in Florida, David Richardson was elected. Mark Ferrandino was chosen by Colorado Democrats to serve as the state's first openly homosexual House speaker. In the State of Oregon, Tina Kotek was elected as the first openly homosexual House speaker. The first openly gay person to serve as a spokesperson for a Republican presidential contender was Richard Grenell, who represented Mitt Romney on foreign affairs during Romney's 2012 campaign for president of the United States. With the passage of this measure, San Francisco will be the first American city to offer and pay for sex reassignment procedures for its transgender residents with no insurance. In the United States, Berkeley, California was the first municipality to declare September 23 as Bisexual Pride and Bi Visibility Day. The first U.S. state to outlaw therapy that purported to make gay persons straight was California. Army Reserve officer Tammy Smith became the first openly gay active military general in American history during a ceremony in Arlington. At a private ceremony held at the Women's Monument in Arlington National Cemetery, Smith received his promotion to brigadier general. The first professional boxer to come out as homosexual was Orlando Cruz. *The Bisexuality Report*, the first of its type to be published in the UK, was released. In this report, Meg Barker (a senior lecturer in psychology at the University of Oxford), Rebecca Jones (a lecturer in health and social care at the University of Oxford), Christina Richards, Helen Bowes-Catton, and Tracey Plowman (of BiUK) compiled research from around the world and made recommendations for bisexual inclusion in the future. At the 2012 World Pride celebration in London, the first International Asexual Conference took place.

In **2013**, same-sex marriage laws were passed in New Zealand, Uruguay, France, Brazil, the U.S. states of Delaware, California, Illinois, Maryland, Oregon, Rhode Island, Minnesota, New Jersey, Hawaii and New Mexico, the Confederated Tribes of the Colville Reservation, the Little Traverse Bay Bands of Odawa Indians, the Pokagon Band of Potawatomi Indians, the Cheyenne and Arapaho Tribes, the Leech Lake Band of Ojibwe, the Grand Portage Band of Chippewa and the Iipay Nation of Santa Ysabel, England and Wales, and the Australian Capital Territory. Section 3 of the *Defense of Marriage Act* was declared unconstitutional by the US Supreme Court, granting same-sex unions legal status. Civil union/registered partnership laws were enacted in the Mexican state of Campeche, and the U.S. State of Colorado. Limited partnership laws were introduced in Costa Rica. Same-sex couple adoption legalization was carried out in New Zealand and France. Ukraine, Montenegro and Curacao held their first pride marches. On January 26, 2013, Kathleen Wynne defeated Sandra Pupatello in the third round of voting for the Ontario Liberal Party's leadership, becoming the first out Gay premier of a Canadian province, Ontario. She became the party's first openly Lesbian leader and the first female premier of Ontario on February 11, 2013. The first openly homosexual prime minister of Luxembourg, Xavier Bettel, and the first openly gay deputy prime minister, Etienne Schneider, both took office on December 4. With Xavier Bettel as Prime Minister and Etienne Schneider as Deputy Prime Minister, Luxembourg became the first nation in the world to have openly homosexual leaders. The first openly transgender Parliamentarian in the UK was Nikki Sinclaire, who came out as transgender. The first British Member of Parliament to come out as bisexual was Daniel Kawczynski. The township of Fresnillo chose Benjamin Medrano as its first openly homosexual mayor in the nation's history. A ministerial meeting on the rights of lesbian, gay, bisexual, and transgender people was convened for the first time at the United Nations. Executive directors of Human Rights Watch and the International Gay and Lesbian Human Rights Commission, along with representatives from the US, France, Argentina, Brazil, Croatia, the Netherlands, Norway, Japan, New Zealand, and the EU, reaffirmed their commitment to collaborating to put an end to discrimination and violence against the LGBT community. Speaking on behalf of the LGBT community, UN High Commissioner for Human Rights Navi Pillay praised the fact that "many countries have embarked on historic reforms—strengthening anti-discrimination laws, combating hate crime against LGBT people, and sensitizing public opinion." In his inaugural address, Barack Obama used the word "gay" and the subject of LGBT rights for the first time in a speech at the American presidential swearing-in. This was the first bi-specific event ever hosted by any White House, and it took place on Celebrate Bisexuality Day. Nearly 30 bisexual advocates attended the closed-door meeting, which allowed them to meet with government representatives and discuss issues of particular importance to the bisexual community. Philip Frank, the husband of Rep. Mark Pocan, became the first same-sex spouse of a federal member to be granted a House Spouse ID. Rep. Jared Polis' (D-Colo.) spouse Marlon Reis received a congressional spouse ID in 2009, but card services later informed him that the designation had been made mistakenly. Nitza Quiñones Alejandro became the first openly homosexual Latina to hold a federal judgeship after being confirmed by the U.S. Senate. As acting secretary of the U.S. Air Force, United States Air Force Under Secretary Eric Fanning became the highest-ranking openly homosexual official in the Department of Defense. Todd Hughes was appointed as the nation's first openly homosexual circuit judge. Robbie Rogers, the first male international association footballer with a complete cap, came out as homosexual on February 15, 2013. He became the first out homosexual male athlete to play in Major League Soccer when he signed with the Los Angeles Galaxy. On April 29, 2013, Jason Collins came out as homosexual in a public setting, making him the first active male professional athlete in a significant North American team sport. Fallon Fox became the first openly transgender athlete in the history of mixed martial arts after coming out as transgender. Jallen Messersmith of Benedictine College in Atchison, Kansas, was thought to be the first openly homosexual basketball player in American men's collegiate history when he came out. Cason Crane accomplished the Seven Summits and carried the rainbow flag to the top of Mount Everest for the first time as an out homosexual man. Liz Carmouche and Jessica Andrade competed in the first UFC bout between two openly homosexual fighters. Darren Young, whose actual name is Fred Rosser, came out as homosexual, becoming the first active professional wrestler to do so. Philadelphia became the first city on the east coast to offer transition-related healthcare to its municipal employees after passing one of the most comprehensive transgender rights acts at the local level, which covered transgender restroom usage and city employee healthcare. U.S. veteran and transgender woman Autumn Sandeen got a letter from a Navy officer stating, "At your request, the Defense Enrollment Eligibility Reporting System (DEERS) has been updated to show your gender as female effective 12 April 2013." According to Outserve representative Allyson Robinson, "To our knowledge, this is the first time that the Department of Defense has acknowledged and validated a change of gender for anybody linked, in a uniformed role — in this case, a military retiree." In 2013, Ben Barres became the first scientist in the US National Academy of Sciences to be publicly transgender. *I Am J* by Cris Beam, which has a transgender theme, was included in the California Department of Education's list of suggested books for grades Pre-K through 12 for the first time. *The School Success and Opportunity Act*, which was passed in California, is the nation's first law protecting transgender students. It states that all public school students in California from kindergarten through 12th grade must be "permitted to participate in sex-segregated school programs and activities, including athletic teams and competitions, and use facilities consistent with his or her gender identity, irrespective of the gender listed on the pupil's records." The world's first publicly transgender billionaire, Jennifer Pritzker, came out as transgender in 2013. The first transgender youngster in Argentina to have her new name legally changed on identification documents was a six-year-old kid named Luana. She was thought to be the youngest person to gain access to the new *Gender Identity Law*, which was enacted in May 2012. The first openly transgender co-chair of GLAAD's National Board of Directors was Jennifer Finney Boylan. Paris Lees made history on October 31, 2013, when she appeared as the first openly transgender panelist on BBC's *Question Time*. Commentators including former deputy prime minister John Prescott and Labour Party deputy leader Harriet Harman praised her for her accomplishment. The first transgender high school coach to come out publicly was Rhode Islander Stephen Alexander. The Montreal-based flight attendants for Air Transat were represented by CUPE 4041, which elected Audrey Gauthier as its president on November 1. As a result, she was chosen as the first openly transgender union local president in Canada. The Australian Senate released its first parliamentary report on the health and human rights of intersex individuals on October 25. The first openly transgender retired Navy SEAL, Kristin Beck (previously Chris Beck), came out. For the first time, the U.S. Department of Veterans Affairs agreed to let a spouse of a soldier be buried at a national cemetery in the country of their service. Linda Campbell, a former Air Force officer, was granted permission by VA Secretary Eric Shinseki to inter her same-sex spouse Nancy Lynchild's ashes in the Willamette National Cemetery in Oregon. Rehana Kausar and Sobia Kamar, both from Pakistan, made history by becoming the first lesbian Muslim couple to legally wed in the UK. The first married homosexual couple to receive approval for a green card was Julian Marsh and Traian Povov. The U.S. Air Force's Join Spouse program made Master Sergeant Angela Shunk and her wife, Tech Sergeant Stacey Shunk, the first same-sex pair to get an assignment together. At the 2013 Eurovision Song Contest, Krista Siegfrids, who sang the song *Marry Me*, closed her performance by kissing one of her female dancers, marking the first time that it had ever happened on a Eurovision stage. Guy Erwin was elected to the Southwest California Synod of the Evangelical Lutheran

Church in America, making him the first openly homosexual ELCA bishop. The winners of the first Bisexual Book Awards were revealed by the Bi Writers Association, which supports bisexual authors, books, and writing, and in the Nuyorican Poets Café in New York City, there was an awards ceremony. Paris Barclay was chosen by the Directors Guild of America to serve as its first openly homosexual and first black president. The smash hit song *Same Love* by Macklemore and Ryan Lewis was the first song to reach the Top 40 in the United States and helped promote and celebrate same-sex unions. The first openly wed homosexual couple in South Korea was comprised of film director Kim Jho Gwang-soo and his lover Kim Seung-hwan, albeit their union was not recognized by the law. The first openly homosexual political figure to appear on an American postage stamp was Harvey Milk. Andy Herren became the first openly homosexual winner of the *Big Brother* reality competition in America. The first same-sex wedding in Romania was broadcast on television. It took place on the reality competition show *Four Weddings and a Challenge* and included two men. When Q Radio initially began broadcasting in September, it made the claim to be India's first radio station dedicated to the needs of lesbians, gays, bisexuals, and transgender persons. A Reform Jewish group called the American Conference of Cantors elected Mark C. Goldman as its first openly homosexual president. The Reconstructionist Rabbinical College's President, Rabbi Deborah Waxman, was chosen. As President of RRC, which served as both a congregational union and a seminary, she was credited with being the first lesbian and female rabbi as well as the first lesbian to head a Jewish seminary. Saul Levin became the first known openly homosexual person to lead the American Psychiatric

Association when he was appointed as the organization's new chief executive officer and medical director on May 15, 2013. Being the highest senior openly homosexual officer in the whole U.S. military at the time, Major General Patricia "Trish" Rose became the first openly lesbian two-star general in the U.S. Air Force. After California, New Jersey became the second state to enact legislation outlawing gay conversion therapy. The first Project Homeless Connect event for lesbian, gay, bisexual, and transgender persons took place in San Francisco. The first bisexual legal professionals, academics, students, and allies national organization in America, known as BiLaw, was established. The diagnosis of hypoactive sexual desire disorder was updated in 2013 to include an exemption for those who self-identify as asexuals in the *Diagnostic and Statistical Manual of Mental Disorders*, Fifth Edition. Raj launched the Indian Asexuals in 2013 as the first initiative for the Indian Asexual and Aromantic Communities. They work through the intersactional feminism lens.

In **2014**, same-sex marriage laws were introduced in Scotland, the US states of Oregon, Pennsylvania, Utah, Illinois, Oklahoma, Virginia, Wisconsin, Indiana, Colorado, Nevada, Idaho, West Virginia, North Carolina, Alaska, Arizona, Wyoming, Kansas, South Carolina, Montana, the Mexican state of Coahuila, the Puyallup Tribe of Indians, the Lac du Flambeau of Lake Superior Chippewa, the Fort McDermitt Paiute and Shoshone Tribes of the Fort McDermitt Indian Reservation, the Fort McDowell Yavapai Nation, the Pascua Yaqui Tribe, the Salt River Pima-Maricopa Indian Community, the San Carlos Apache Tribe, the Wind River Indian Reservation, the Blackfoot Tribe and the Keweenaw Bay Indian Community, Luxembourg, England and Wales. Civil union/registered partnership laws were passed in Estonia, Gibraltar (with joint adoption), Malta (with joint adoption) and Croatia. Same-sex couple adoption legislation came into being in Andorra, and the Mexican state of Coahuila. Northern Cyprus and Palau decriminalized homosexuality. The Canadian province of Saskatchewan passed anti-discrimination laws to fight discrimination on the basis of gender identity. The first same-sex couple in Mississippi to legally wed was Anna Guillot and Chrissy Kelly, who were wed in New York in 2012. They established a public record of their union. Unfortunately, in Mississippi, this did not make their marriage valid. Giuseppe Chigiotti and Stefano Bucci's 2012 marriage in New York was the first international same-sex union to receive legal recognition in Italy. An Italian court for the first time authorized the adoption of a kid residing with a gay couple. One of the women in the pair was the biological mother of the kid, and her partner was given legal permission to adopt the child and become her co-parent. The first lesbian cemetery in the world opened in Berlin, Germany. The first lesbian couple's kid to be christened by the Catholic Church in Argentina was Umma Azul. Emilia Maria Jesty, a lesbian couple's child, was the first person to be born in Tennessee with a woman identified as her "father" on the birth certificate. Tracy Dice Johnson, who was the first-known same-sex war widow, received survivor benefits after her wife Donna Johnson was killed in a suicide bombing in 2012. For the first time ever, an Australian birth certificate indicated that both members of a same-sex relationship were the legal parents of a kid at birth when both lesbian parents are named on the birth certificates of their children. A 49-year-old Pentagon employee and partner named David Bucher were married at the U.S. Naval Academy Chapel's first-ever same-sex ceremony. The United States Equal Employment Opportunity Commission initiated the first Title VII action on behalf of transgender employees. Amiee Stephens and Brandi Branson, two transgender individuals, were the plaintiffs in the cases. The Working Mother of the Year award was given to Meghan Stabler, the first openly transgender woman. Laverne Cox was interviewed for the story "The Transgender Tipping Point" which appeared on the cover of *Time* magazine on June 9, 2014. Also, she made history by being the first openly transgender person to be nominated for an Emmy in the acting category for her performance as Sophia Burset in *Orange Is the New Black*. In the United States, Mount Holyoke was the first Seven Sisters institution to welcome transgender students, while Mills College was the first single-sex institution to do so. The first openly transgender high school homecoming king in North Carolina was Blake Brockington. Trans Lifeline, the first suicide hotline in the United States specifically for transgender persons, was developed by Nina Chaubal and Greta Gustava Martela. The first openly transgender African-American woman to perform at Carnegie Hall was Tona Brown. Susan Stryker and Paisley Currah served as coeditors for *Transgender Studies Quarterly*, the first academic journal not focused on medicine to address transgender concerns. The Transgender Trends panel at San Diego Comic-Con was the convention's first discussion of the topic. Mikayla Connell, who was openly transgender, became the first transgender police officer to graduate from the San Francisco Police Academy. In honor of transgender pioneer Vicki Marlane, the 100 block of Turk Street in San Francisco was renamed Vicki Mar Lane. Lea T became the first openly transgender model to represent a major cosmetics company after landing the role of Redken, an

American haircare company. Jennifer Barge, who was openly transgender, served as the spokeswoman for a nationwide Centers for Disease Control and Prevention campaign for the first time. Chris Mosier was inducted into the National Gay and Lesbian Sports Hall of Fame as the first openly transgender man. At the 2014 Gay Games, Kinnon MacKinnon won gold in powerlifting as the first openly transgender man. *Boy Meets Girl*, the first transgender sitcom produced in Britain, was commissioned by BBC2. It centered on the relationship between Leo, a 26-year-old trans man, and Judy, a 40-year-old trans woman. ICEIS Rain made history by being the first openly two-spirit performer at the Aboriginal Peoples Choice Music Awards. As India's first openly transgender television news anchor, Padmini Prakash made history. The diagnosis of Gender Identity Disorder was eliminated as a prerequisite for the gender recognition procedure in Denmark, making it the first nation in Europe to do so. Gender identification was included in Malta's constitution as a protected class for the first time in European history. Malta saw the wedding of the first openly transgender lady. To commemorate a year since their third gender was officially acknowledged by the government, at least 1,000 openly transgender Bangladeshis participated in the country's first pride march. The kicker at Willamette University, Conner Mertens, came out as bisexual and became the first active college football player to identify as LGBT. Derrick Gordon, a basketball player at UMass, came out and became the first out homosexual college basketball player in Division I. The St. Louis Rams selected Michael Sam, making him the first out homosexual athlete ever selected for the National Football League. The first transgender student-athlete to represent Arizona in a winter sport has been given permission by the Arizona Interscholastic Association Executive Board. The first active Division I football player to come out as homosexual was Edward Sarafin, a reserve offensive lineman at Arizona State. Rob Kearney, a professional strongman, became the first out homosexual man to actively compete in professional, international strongman events after coming out as gay. The FTM Fitness World Bodybuilding Competition, the first bodybuilding contest for transgender men, was held in conjunction with the FTM Fitness Conference. In Division I men's basketball, Derrick Gordon became the first out homosexual player to take the court. Dale Scott became the first out homosexual umpire in Major League Baseball in 2014 after coming out as gay. When the LA Galaxy won the Major League Soccer Cup in 2014, Robbie Rogers made history by being the first out gay male athlete to take home a major team pro sports championship in the United States. The Disney Channel's *Good Luck Charlie* made history by featuring a same-sex relationship for the first time; Susan and Cheryl played the pair. Tom of Finland, a well-known homoerotic artist, was honored on stamps released by Finland. The Amsterdam Pride Canal Parade included the first Jewish boat. The lone rabbi on board was Marianne van Praag, a Reform rabbi from The Hague. Another participant in the Amsterdam Pride Canal Parade was the first Moroccan boat. For the first time in its history, the women's magazine *Cosmopolitan* gave lesbians sex tips. The first openly homosexual Boy Scout to earn the rank of Eagle Scout was 17-year-old Pascal Tessier from Chevy Chase, Maryland. As a fourth-tier silver sponsor of Gay Games 9, the United Church of Christ was the first religious organization to support the event heavily. After being named the Rose of

Tralee, Maria Walsh came out as homosexual, making her the first openly gay Rose of Tralee. *My Chacha Is Gay*," written by Canadian-born author and illustrator Eiynah, was published in print in 2014 after being originally published online. It was the first children's book in Pakistan to address homophobia. In Tel Aviv, a memorial to LGBT individuals persecuted by the Nazis was inaugurated in 2014. It was Israel's first official acknowledgment of non-Jewish Holocaust victims. The first openly homosexual man to be ordained as a Conservative Jewish Rabbi was Mikie Goldstein. After being appointed as the synagogue's spiritual leader in Rehovot, Mikie Goldstein became the first out homosexual congregational rabbi in the Israeli Conservative movement (Congregation Adat Shalom-Emanuel). In its November 2014 edition, *Family Circle* published a same-sex couple for the first time. The song *Era Diferente* (meaning She Was Different), about a lesbian teen who falls in love with her best friend, was included on the Los Tigres del Norte album *Realidades* in 2014. According to the band's lead singer and songwriter Jorge Hernandez, this was the first time a norteño group had ever written a gay love song. On September 26, 2014, the UN Human Rights Council adopted a second resolution concerning gender identity and sexual orientation. It was the first time in the Council's history that it passed a resolution on LGBT rights with a majority of its members, passing by a vote of 25 to 14. The first openly homosexual person to be appointed to a cabinet position in any African country was Lynne Brown, who was selected as the first openly gay cabinet minister in South Africa. Zakhcle Mbhele became the first openly homosexual black member of parliament in any African country when he was elected to the South African parliament. Petra De Sutter became the first openly transgender person to hold a position in the Senate of Belgium's Parliament. In the northwest Peruvian province of Trujillo, Luisa Revilla Urcia was elected to the municipal council and made history as the nation's first openly transgender person. Subsequently, Carlos Bruce came out, making him the country of Peru's first openly homosexual congressman. Edgars Rinkēvičs became the most well-known openly gay politician in a former Soviet Bloc nation after becoming the first MP in Latvia to come out as homosexual. Robert Biedroń, who was elected mayor of Supsk, became Poland's first openly homosexual mayor. The first openly homosexual judge to hold a position on the High Court bench in New Zealand, Matthew Muir, was sworn in. Martin Foley was named Minister of Equality by the Labor government in Victoria, Australia, becoming the first government in Australian history to have a specific Minister in charge of matters pertaining to gay, lesbian, bisexual, transgender, and intersex people. Andrew Barr was sworn in as the Australian Capital Territory's (ACT) chief minister, making him the country's first out homosexual state government leader. Maite Oronoz Rodriguez was the first openly homosexual candidate to be nominated for a position on the Supreme Court of Puerto Rico. She was confirmed for the position later that year. The first openly homosexual African-American man to be confirmed as a federal judge in the United States was Darrin P. Gayles. The Senate approved Judith Ellen Levy to become Michigan's first openly lesbian federal judge. As the first openly lesbian speaker of the California Legislature, Toni Atkins was chosen. She took on the role of acting governor for the day. The first national campaign commercial for an American office to include a same-sex pair was broadcast by Monica Wehby (Ben West and Paul Rummell). Jim Ferlo came out as gay, making him the first openly gay senator from Pennsylvania. Maura Healey was elected in Massachusetts to become the nation's first out homosexual state attorney general. Aditi Hardikar was appointed as the White House's official liaison to the LGBT community, making her the first woman of color to hold that position. She took over for Monique Dorsainvil, who had been acting as the interim liaison following Gautam Raghavan's resignation. The first openly transgender elected politician in Wisconsin, Gypsy Vered Meltzer, was elected to the Appleton City Council. The LGBT pride flag was flown at the presidential palace in Costa Rica; according to the International Gay and Lesbian Human Rights Commission, this was the first time in the Americas that such a flag has been flown from a head of the state's office. Several thousands of people participated in the first LGBT pride march ever held in Cyprus. The first international symposium on LGBTQ rights was held in Hong Kong. Mauricio Ruiz made his sexual orientation public for the first time while a serving member of the Chilean military. In the United States, California became the first state to formally outlaw the use of transgender and gay panic defenses in murder cases. When its stock was made available for trading in August 2014, Florida-based bank C1 Financial made history as the first publicly traded bank in the country to have an openly gay CEO (Trevor Burgess). Apple Inc. CEO Tim Cook came out as gay, making him the first openly gay CEO to be on the *Fortune 500* list. The first LGBT organization in history to march in Boston's Veterans Day parade was a delegation of the nonprofit OutVets. With the theme "Bi the Way, Our Health Matters Too!", the Boston, Massachusetts-based Bisexual Resource Center designated March 2014 as the first Bisexual Health Awareness Month. This initiative featured the first social media campaign to address disparities in physical and mental health that the bisexual community faces. The London Lesbian and Gay Switchboard's 40-year history received recognition from Queen Elizabeth II, which was the first time the Monarch ever openly backed the LGBT community. The Queen left a message for them, wishing everyone involved "Best wishes and congratulations on this very special anniversary."

In **2015**, same-sex marriage laws were passed in Finland, Ireland, the United States, the Central Council of the Tlingit and Haida Tribes of Alaska, the Oneida Nation of Wisconsin, the Confederated Tribes of Siletz Indians, the Mexican states of Chihuahua, Guerrero and Nayarit, and Luxembourg (with joint adoption). Civil union/registered partnership laws were passed in Chile, Ecuador (expansion), Cyprus, and Greece. Same-sex couple adoption legislation was adopted in Austria and Ireland. Mozambique decriminalized homosexuality. The Canadian province of Alberta passed anti-discrimination laws to discourage discrimination on the basis of gender identity and gender expression. When Madhu Kinnar was elected mayor of Chhattisgarh's Raigarh Municipal Corporation, she made history as the nation's first openly transgender mayor. Leo Varadkar, Ireland's health minister, came out as homosexual, making him the country's first openly gay government official ever. On February 21, Canadian politician Wade MacLauchlan was elected leader of the ruling Prince Edward Island Liberal Party. On February 23, he took the oath of office becoming Canada's second openly homosexual and first openly gay male provincial premier. Later, on May 4, his party won the provincial election, making him the first openly gay member of Prince Edward Island's Legislative Assembly. As the first three openly LGBT MLAs in the province, Michael Connolly, Ricardo Miranda, and Estefania Cortes-Vargas were elected to the Legislative Assembly of Alberta. Later coming out as genderqueer, Cortes-Vargas became the first openly trans person to hold elected office in Canada. The first democratic constitution in Asia to particularly safeguard the rights of lesbian, gay, bisexual, and transgender minorities was enacted by Nepal. Tamara Adrián was chosen to serve in the Venezuelan National Assembly, making her both the first openly transgender person to serve in the Western Hemisphere's national legislature and the first transgender person to serve in Venezuela. As the new president and CEO of the Victory Fund, Aisha Moodie-Mills became the first woman, first black woman, first lesbian, and first black lesbian to hold that position in a major national LGBT organization. Mark B. Cohen, a state representative from Pennsylvania, introduced the state's first transgender rights legislation. As governor of Oregon, Kate Brown made history by being the first openly bisexual governor in the country. As Salt Lake City's first openly homosexual mayor, Jackie Biskupski won the election. Nancy VanReece became Tennessee's first openly lesbian legislator when she won the Metro Council District 8 seat in Nashville. As manager of Hillary Clinton's presidential campaign, Robby Mook made history by being the first out homosexual campaign manager. As the first Special Envoy for the Human Rights of LGBT Persons, Randy Berry was appointed. The terms "lesbian," "bisexual," and "transgender" were first used by President Barack Obama in a State of the Union address. Raffi Freedman-Gurspan became the first openly transgender employee of the White

House when President Obama hired her to work as an Outreach and Recruitment Director in the Presidential Personnel Office. The first LGBT publication in Cambodia was *Q Cambodia*. For the first time, Jamaica conducted LGBT Pride events. The first openly transgender television reporter on American national television, Zoey Tur joined *Inside Edition* as a Special Correspondent in February. When Thomas Roberts hosted NBC's *Nightly News* for a day, he made history by being the first out homosexual evening news anchor on network television. The first same-sex couple to exchange vows on cable television was Lance Bass and Michael Turchin. The lead character of The 100, Clarke Griffin (played by Eliza Taylor), was revealed by screenwriter Jason Rothenberg to be openly bisexual, making her the first such figure on the CW network. Boston Pride and OutVets, the city's first homosexual organizations, participated in the St. Patrick's Day parade. An organization of LGBT NBCUniversal employees named OUT@NBCUniversal made history by being the first openly gay organization to march in the St. Patrick's Day parade in New York City. The D.C. Center for the LGBT Community became the first homosexual organization to march in the St. Patrick's Day parade in Washington, D.C. A resolution lifting the ban on openly homosexual adult leaders and staff was approved by the Boy Scouts' National Executive Board. When he was hired by the Boy Scouts of America's Greater New York Councils, Pascal Tessier made history as the first openly homosexual adult Boy Scout in the country to work as a summer camp director. Patricia Velásquez's memoir *Straight Walk*, which was published in February 2015, recounts her experiences as a child growing up in poverty in Venezuela and how her friendship with Sandra Bernhard helped her come to terms with the fact that she was a lesbian. She became the first out gay Latina supermodel in the world as a result. The Rev. Ángel David Marrero, the first openly homosexual (Caribbean) Hispanic to be ordained in this denomination, received his pastorate from the Evangelical Lutheran Church in America in April 2015. In the May 2015 edition of *Vogue*, Andreja Pejic was the magazine's first openly transgender model to be profiled. Laverne Cox was the first openly transgender actress to pose naked for the annual "Nudes" edition of *Allure*. Together with that, she made history by becoming the first openly transgender person to have a wax replica of herself at Madame Tussauds. In her capacity as Executive Producer of *Laverne Cox Presents: The T Word*, she also received a Daytime Emmy Award for Outstanding Special Class Special. *The T Word* was the first transgender documentary to win a Daytime Emmy, and she became the first openly transgender woman to do so in the role of Executive Producer. The first openly transgender woman to appear on the cover of *Vanity Fair* was Caitlyn Jenner. Broadway saw the debut of *Fun Home*, the first musical with a lesbian lead character. In the Abraham Lincoln National Cemetery in Elwood, Illinois, the first memorial honoring LGBT veterans to receive government approval in the United States was erected. The Stonewall Inn was the first municipal location to be taken into consideration solely for its significance to the LGBT community when the New York City Landmarks Preservation Commission said on May 29, 2015 that it would formally consider designating it as a landmark. The Stonewall Inn became the first monument to be recognized for its contribution to the battle for gay rights when the New York City Landmarks Preservation Commission unanimously approved its designation as a municipal landmark on June 23, 2015. The

Royal Vauxhall Tavern was the first structure in the UK to receive a special "listing" status because of its LGBT heritage; the Department of Culture, Media, and Sport of the UK gave it a Grade II listed status. The *Purple List*, the first list of its kind, was produced by the British bisexual women's website *Biscuit* in order to honor bisexuals who have worked to combat biphobia and raise awareness of the community. With his co-winner Diane Anderson-Minshall, Jacob Anderson-Minshall became the first openly transgender author to get a Goldie award from the Golden Crown Literary Society for their book *Queerly Beloved: A Love Story Beyond Genders*. The first openly transgender houseguest on the American television show *Big Brother* was Audrey Middleton. With his portrayal of Nick in the drama *The Bold and the Beautiful*, Scott Turner Schofield made history as the first out transgender actor to have a significant role on daytime television. When Karla Mosley's character Maya Avant wed Rick Forrester (played by Jacob Young) on the same show, she made television history as the first transgender bride. The first openly transgender model to be signed by IMG was Hari Nef. When serving as a guest presenter on *The Project*, Andrew Guy made history as Australia's first openly transgender TV host. Scottish LGBTI Awards conducted their first event. As the first out homosexual man to host the *Academy Awards*, Neil Patrick Harris made history. For the actors Kitana Kiki Rodriguez and Mya Taylor in the film *Tangerine*, the first Oscar campaigns for openly transgender actresses were launched with the backing of a film producer. Riley Carter Millington was cast in *EastEnders* as "Kyle," a character who transitioned from female to male, just as Riley did in real life. Riley became the first openly transgender actor in UK TV television drama history. Soon after, transgender actress Annie Wallace was cast in *Hollyoaks*. The first openly bisexual woman and CEO of Lloyd's of London, Inga Beale, was named number one on the *OUTstanding & Financial Times* Leading LGBT executive power list. Loiza Lamers became the first openly transgender winner of the "Top Model" franchise after she won *Holland's Next Top Model*. Mya Taylor became the first openly transgender actor to get a *Gotham Award* when she won the Breakthrough Actor category. The Central Conference of American Rabbis, the oldest and biggest rabbinical organization in North America, elected Rabbi Denise Eger as its first openly LGBT president in March 2015. Abby Stein, who got her rabbinical degree in 2011 at Yeshiva Viznitz in South Fallsburg, New York, became the first openly transgender woman (and the first woman) to have been ordained by an ultra-Orthodox institution after coming out as transgender. Nevertheless, this was before she came out as transgender, and as of 2016, she was no longer employed as a rabbi. She was also the first openly transgender person raised in a Hasidic neighborhood and a direct descendant of the Baal Shem Tov, who founded Hasidic Judaism. The first male same-sex couple selected to exchange the first kiss when a U.S. Navy ship arrived was Thomas Sawicki and Shawn Brier. By being married at Full Sutton Prison in East Yorkshire, Mikhail Ivan Gallatinov and Mark Goodwin were the first couple to hold a same-sex wedding in a UK prison. By allowing a lesbian couple and their son's biological father, who provided sperm for their pregnancy, to be included on the child's birth certificate, Argentina became the first country in Latin America to acknowledge same-sex partners and biological parents. The child's name was Antonio, and his parents were Hernan Melazzi, Valeria

Gaete, and Susana Guichal. When President Obama declared May as National Foster Care Month, he made history as the first president to clearly state that gender identity should not be a barrier to adoption or foster parenthood. Upon their graduation from the Boston Police Academy, Shawn MacIver and James Moccia made history as the first openly homosexual couple to complete a police academy together. The first place in Japan, or anywhere in East Asia, to recognize same-sex partnerships was the Shibuya ward of Tokyo, which approved municipal legislation providing same-sex couples the right to partnership certificates. By popular choice, Ireland became the first nation to formally recognize same-sex unions. On February 12, 2015, *USA Today* reported that the Fort Leavenworth commandant had stated in a memo dated February 5 that he had "approved adding hormone treatment to Inmate Chelsea Manning's treatment plan after carefully considering the recommendation that hormone treatment is medically appropriate and necessary, and weighing all associated safety and security risks presented." According to *USA Today*, Chelsea Manning continued to serve as a soldier, and the U.S. Army's choice to provide her with hormone medication was a first. As a first for the state, a federal court mandated that Michelle-Lael Norsworthy, a transgender prisoner, be allowed access to gender-affirming surgery by the California Department of Corrections. During Women's History Month, the first White House briefing for trans women of color took place. The United States of America v. Southeastern Oklahoma State University and the Regional University System of Oklahoma lawsuit was filed in federal court in the state of Oklahoma and was the first civil action the U.S. Justice Department had brought on behalf of a transgender individual (Rachel Tudor). Utah's first openly transgender prom queen, Maka Brown, an 18-year-old senior at the Salt Lake School for Performing Arts, won the title. A first-of-its-kind booklet, *Schools In Transition: A Guide for Supporting Transgender Students in K–12 Schools*, was released with information on how to create welcoming settings for all transgender kids in kindergarten through twelfth grade. For the first time, Philadelphia hoisted the transgender pride flag above City Hall. Manabi Bandopadhyay started working as the principal of the Krishnagar Women's College in the Nadia district. She was the country's first openly transgender college principal. The Channel 4 program *Girls to Men* featured the first transgender man's phalloplasty ever to be captured on video. The first US legislative forum on violence against transgender people took place this same year. The first clinic for transgender military members was established by the US Department of Veterans Affairs. As part of a special collector's edition, Aydian Dowling became the first openly transgender guy to appear on the cover of *Men's Health*. Malta was the first nation in the world to ban sterilization and intrusive surgery on intersex persons in April 2015. Adrianna Vorderbruggen, who died in battle, was said to be the first openly homosexual American officer in the Air Force and the first female active-duty military member to die in battle. Michael Sam became the first out homosexual player in the history of the CFL on May 22, 2015, when he signed a two-year deal with the Montreal Alouettes. On August 7, 2015, Michael Sam made his CFL debut against the Ottawa Redblacks, making him the league's first out homosexual player to take the field in a regular-season contest. In the game, he did not register a tackle. When Chris Mosier gained a spot on Team USA in the men's sprint duathlon, he became the first known openly trans athlete to join a U.S. national team that matched his gender identification rather than the gender assigned to him at birth. Sean Conroy, who pitched nine scoreless innings for the Sonoma Stompers in their 7-0 victory over the Vallejo Admirals in the Pacific Association of Baseball Clubs, an independent league with teams from Northern California, made history by becoming the first openly gay baseball player to play in a professional game. A New Zealander named Benjamin Thomas Watt made history as the first out homosexual professional boxing judge. David Denson became the first active minor league baseball player connected to a Major League Baseball team to come out as homosexual when he did so. The first homosexual professional rugby league player in Britain was Keegan Hirst. Sam Stanley, Joe Stanley's nephew, was the first gay rugby union player in England. The first openly homosexual coach in Division I men's basketball was Chris Burns, an assistant coach at Bryant University who came out as gay. Breanna Sinclairé sang the national anthem at a Major League Baseball game, making her the first openly transgender person to do so. Phuti Lekoloane, the first openly homosexual male football player in South Africa, came out. In 2015, George Norman ran for municipal office as the country's first openly asexual candidate.

In **2016**, same-sex marriage laws were passed in Colombia, Isle of Man, the Mexican states of Jalisco, Campeche, Colima, Michoacán and Morelos, Greenland, Gibraltar, British Antarctic Territory, Faroe Islands, Guernsey, and Ascension Island. Civil union/registered partnership laws were enacted in Italy, Aruba and Estonia. Same-sex couple adoption legislation was introduced in Portugal. Seychelles, Nauru and Belize decriminalized homosexuality. Anti-discrimination laws prohibiting discrimination on the basis of gender identity and gender expression were adopted in the Canadian provinces of Quebec and British Columbia. Adidas revealed an LGBT provision in athletes' contracts on February 11th, 2016. The first openly transgender woman to appear on the cover of *Women's Running* was Amelia Gapin. Chris Mosier was the first publicly transgender athlete to appear in the "Body Issue" of *ESPN The Magazine* and the first openly transgender athlete to appear in a Nike advertisement. Caitlyn Jenner made history by being the first openly transgender person on the cover of *Sports Illustrated*. The first openly homosexual champion in UFC history was Amanda Nunes. The National Women's Hockey League player Harrison Browne became the first openly transgender athlete in professional American team sports when he came out as a transgender guy. Lea T led the Brazilian team into the stadium on her bike at the 2016 Rio Olympics, making history as the first openly transgender person to take part in an Olympics opening ceremony. Kate and Helen Richardson-Walsh were the first same-sex married pair to win an Olympic medal when the British women's field hockey team won the gold medal at the games. Kate and Helen were both members of that squad. Adam Price, Jeremy Miles, and Hannah Blythyn were the first openly homosexual Assembly members from Wales. Justine Greening, a minister in the British government, came out as being in a same-sex relationship and became the first openly LGB female cabinet minister. Anwen Muston became the first openly transgender woman to be elected as a Labour representative when she won a seat on Wolverhampton City Council. When Prince William graced the cover of the July issue of *Attitude*, he made history as the first member of the British royal family to do so. In the cover story, he also made history as the first British royal to publicly denounce bullying of the homosexual community. Lord Ivar Mountbatten came out as homosexual and disclosed that he was seeing James Coyle, the head of airline cabin services, whom he had met at a Verbier ski resort. He was the first member of the extended family to come out as gay while not being a member of the British royal family. The first openly homosexual Lord Mayor of Manchester was sworn in as Carl Austin-Behan. At Glasgow Pride 2017, Nicola Sturgeon made history by being the first UK prime minister or first minister to give a speech at a gay pride celebration. She addressed the gathering and promised to keep working for respect and equality in the UK, concluding with the phrase "Love is Love." Raffi Freedman-Gurspan was the first openly transgender person to be named as the White House's primary LGBT liaison by President Barack Obama. Maite Oronoz Rodríguez became the first openly homosexual top justice in American history and the first chief justice of Puerto Rico. The United States Army's first out homosexual secretary is Eric Fanning. The transgender pride flag was raised by Santa Clara County for the first time as a county government in the United States. The first organization of its type, Trans United Fund was established as a 501(c)(4) nonprofit of transgender leaders with a focus on transgender problems. For the US House of Representatives, Misty Plowright made history by being the first openly transgender candidate to prevail in a major party primary. For the US Senate, Misty Snow became the first openly transgender candidate to prevail in a major party primary. The first openly homosexual person to serve on the Republican Party's Platform Committee was Rachel

Hoff, who did so during the GOP Convention. Peter Thiel was the first to publicly acknowledge his sexual orientation in a speech. In his acceptance speech at the 2016 Republican National Convention on July 21, 2016, Donald Trump made history by becoming the first Republican nominee to mention the LGBT community in a GOP nomination address. He said, "As your president, I will do everything in my power to protect our LGBTQ citizens from the violence and oppression of a hateful foreign ideology." The first openly transgender speaker to address a major party conference in American history was Sarah McBride, who spoke during the Democratic National Convention. Being the first presumed presidential contender from any major party to participate in the NYC Pride March, Hillary Clinton authored an opinion piece for *Philadelphia Gay News*, marking the first time a major-party presidential candidate did so. Anderson Cooper and Martha Raddatz moderated the second presidential debate between Donald Trump and Hillary Clinton. He became the first out homosexual moderator of a presidential debate as a result. As governor of Oregon, Kate Brown made history by being the first openly bisexual governor in the history of the United States (and indeed the first openly LGBT person elected as such). Jokowi, the president of Indonesia, said that LGBT rights should be protected in his country. The first openly lesbian minister of Ireland was Katherine Zappone. Two openly homosexual men ran for parliament in Russia for the first time. The Sydney Gay and Lesbian Mardi Gras was attended by both Bill Shorten, the leader of the opposition, and Australian Prime Minister Malcolm Turnbull, making him the first incumbent prime minister to do so. When Guðni Th. Jóhannesson, the president of Iceland, gave a speech during Reykjavík Pride

2016, he made history by being the first head of state to take part in a pride march. Justin Trudeau, the prime minister of Canada, made history by marching in a pride parade. Geraldine Roman was the first openly transgender person in the Philippines to be elected to Congress. For the first time, the UN Security Council used language to recognize violence against the LGBT community when it denounced the Orlando nightclub attack. Activists flew the first pride flag into the Stratosphere in August using a high-altitude balloon, which traveled 21.1 miles (34.1 km). President Barack Obama officially designated the Stonewall National Monument on June 24, 2016, making it the first National Monument recognized as an LGBT historic place in the country. The Stonewall Inn, Christopher Street Park, and the section of Christopher Street that borders the park are all included in the status of a National Monument. When the Furies Collective's residence at 219 11th St. SE was unanimously approved for inclusion in the D.C. Inventory of Historic Places, it was designated as the city's first lesbian-related historic site. The first Hispanic LGBT site to be included on the National Register of Historic Places is Edificio Comunidad de Orgullo Gay. On August 16, 2016, the USNS Harvey Milk received its official name at a ceremony in San Francisco. It was the first ship in the U.S. Navy to bear the name of an out homosexual leader (Harvey Milk, who served as a diving officer in the Navy from 1951 to 1955). Mya Taylor received the Best Supporting Female Independent Spirit Award, becoming her the first openly transgender performer to do so. Erin O'Flaherty became the first openly lesbian Miss America contender and the first openly homosexual Miss Missouri. Aaron Devor was selected as the inaugural chair after Jennifer Pritzker donated $2 million through her foundation to establish the first endowed academic chair of transgender studies in the world at the University of Victoria in British Columbia. The creation of the first LGBT human rights monitor was approved by the UN. Nur Warsame became Australia's first openly homosexual Imam after coming out. Karen Oliveto was chosen as the first openly homosexual bishop in the United Methodist church. The first bishop in the Church of England to come out as gay was Nicholas Chamberlain, who did so in response to threats of an outing from an anonymous Sunday newspaper. He said that in accordance with the Bishops' regulations, which state that gay clergy must practice abstinence and are not permitted to marry, he cohabited with his lover in a celibate same-sex relationship. The first animated married same-sex pair appeared on a Nickelodeon program called *The Loud House*. Hari Nef was the first openly transgender woman to appear on the cover of a major commercial British magazine when *Elle* created special collectors' covers for their September 2016 edition. The first two openly transgender models to grace a *Harper's Bazaar* cover were Tracey Norman and Geena Rocero. Hugo Alcalde of Chile became the first openly homosexual police officer to get into a civil union in that nation. "To Connect And Inspire" was the theme of the first World LGBT Conference for Criminal Justice Professionals, which took place in August of this year. On August 16, 2016, the USNS Harvey Milk received its official name at a ceremony in San Francisco. The Chilean Ministry of Health mandated in January 2016 that all needless normalization procedures, including irreversible surgery for intersex children, be stopped until they are old enough to make their own decisions. The first openly transgender woman to receive the International Women of Courage Award was

Nisha Ayub in 2016. Gavin Grimm, a transgender male student, won a significant legal victory in April 2016 when the 4th U.S. Circuit Court of Appeals decided in his favor. This was the first decision by a U.S. appeals court concluding that transgender students are protected under federal laws that forbid sex-based discrimination. The decision was made in response to an appeal of the Gloucester County School Board's rule requiring transgender pupils to use alternative restrooms. On June 30, 2016, it was stated that effective that day, transgender United States service personnel who otherwise met eligibility requirements may no longer be discharged, refused reenlistment, involuntarily separated from duty or denied continuation of service. The first transgender beauty contest in Israel, "Miss Trans Israel," took place at a Tel Aviv nightclub. For the first time, two men exchanged the traditional first kiss that a sailor and their spouse exchanged after serving in the Canadian Navy on active service. The first same-sex wedding in Cyprus was celebrated by an unnamed couple, while Marios Frixou and Fanos Eleftheriades were married in front of the public for the first time. The first same-sex union in a federal immigration detention facility in the United States took place between Tom Swann and Guillermo Hernandez. Rabbi Karina Finkielstein administered the first Jewish same-sex wedding ceremony in Latin America, which took place in Buenos Aires between Victoria Escobar and Romina Charur. A lesbian couple was granted legal adoption of each other's biological children in Italy's first instance. The first same-sex marriage in the Isle of Man was between Luke Carine and Zak Tomlinson. Both pro-marriage and anti-marriage equality protests took place in Mexico. On Ketagalan Boulevard, the major thoroughfare outside the presidential office in Taipei, Taiwan, 250,000 pro-gay marriage demonstrators assembled. The first openly asexual state election candidate in the US was Joe Parrish in 2016.

In **2017**, same-sex marriage laws were passed in Ascension Island, Austria (to take effect by 1 January 2019), Taiwan (to take effect by 24 May 2019), Faroe Islands, Finland, Alderney, Australia, Bermuda (temporarily repealed from 2 June 2018 – 23 November 2018), Germany, Guernsey, Falkland Islands, Malta, Saint Helena, Tristan da Cunha, and the Mexican states of Chiapas, Baja California and Puebla. With the passage of *Bill C-16* in Canada, which forbade discrimination against trans people and acknowledged bias against trans people as an aggravating factor in crime (hate crime), the province of New Brunswick and the territories of Nunavut and Yukon also passed legislation prohibiting discrimination against trans people and allowing individuals to change their legal gender without surgery. As a result, trans people were protected from discrimination in all provinces and territories. The Supreme Court of India ruled that the right to privacy was inherently protected under *Article 21* and *Part 3* of the *Indian Constitution* and criticized the reasoning behind the earlier 2013 Supreme Court decision in Koushal v. Naz Foundation, which reinstated *Section 377* of the *Indian Penal Code* and dismissed LGBT rights as "so-called" and belonging to "a minuscule fraction of the country's population." The new decision recognized sexual orientation alongside "protection of personal intimacies," "family life, marriage, procreation, the home", and "a right to be left alone" as a fundamental "sanctity" of privacy. The decision gave ground for a more robust legal challenge to *Section 377*. Le Fou, who appeared in the 2017 live-action *Beauty and the Beast* version, was gay, making him the first openly gay character in a Disney movie. The first openly homosexual singer to make a musical breakthrough in Korea was Marshall Bang. Avery Jackson, a 9-year-old transgender girl, was on the cover of the January 2017 issue of *National Geographic*, making her the publication's first openly transgender cover model. The Mystery Writers of America designated openly lesbian author Ellen Hart as a Grand Master, making her the first openly LGBT author to receive this honor. Joseph Maldonado joined the Boy Scouts of America as the organization's first openly transgender member. He was turned down by the Cub Scouts in 2016 due to his gender identity, but when his story went viral in 2017, the policy was amended. The role she played in *Those Who Make Revolution Halfway Only Dig Their Own Graves* (Ceux qui font les révolutions à moitié n'ont fait que se creuser un tombeau) earned Gabrielle Tremblay the distinction of being the first openly transgender actress to be nominated for a Canadian Screen Award for Best Supporting Actress. Valentina Sampaio, a Brazilian model, made history by being the first openly transgender person to grace the cover of *French Vogue*. During the Grammy Awards, Martina Robledo made history by being the first openly transgender woman to present a prize. The first LGBT-related movie to win Best Picture at the Oscars was *Moonlight*. M. Barclay was appointed as a deacon in the United Methodist Church for the first time as an openly non-binary trans person. The first publicly transgender gondolier in Venice was Alex Hai, who came out as a transgender man. The first out homosexual referee in English soccer history was Ryan Atkin. Katie Sowers, an assistant coach with the San Francisco 49ers, came out as homosexual, making her the first openly LGBT coach in the NFL and in all of the American men's professional sports. Scott Frantz made history by playing for an NCAA Division I Football Bowl Subdivision school as the first out homosexual college football player. The first religious gathering in West Africa that welcomed LGBT people took place in August 2017. The Interfaith Diversity Network of West Africa hosted an interfaith diversity event with the theme "Building Bridges, Sharing Stories, Creating Hope" that attracted over 30 participants from ten West African nations, including Benin, Nigeria, Ghana, Sierra Leone, Liberia, The Gambia, Burkina Faso, Côte d'Ivoire, Mali, and Togo. The first fashion designer to introduce a rainbow hijab was MOGA, a Muslim women's clothing line. New Hope's mayor, Jess Herbst, came out as transgender, making her the first openly transgender elected official in Texas history. Tomoya Hosoda was elected to serve as a councilor for the city of Iruma, making Japan the first nation in the world to elect an openly transgender man to a position of public trust. In the Office for Civil Rights of the US Department of Education, Candice Jackson was nominated as the organization's first openly gay Deputy Assistant Secretary for Strategic Operations and Outreach. Christopher Constant and Felix Rivera, the first openly LGBT elected politicians in Alaska, were both chosen for the Anchorage Assembly. The first openly homosexual directly elected metro mayor in the UK was Andy Street. After receiving 51 out of the 73 votes in the parliamentary party, Leo Varadkar was elected to serve as the subsequent Taoiseach (Prime Minister) of Ireland and head of the Fine Gael party. In addition to being the youngest and first Taoiseach of half-Indian origin, he was also the first out homosexual Taoiseach. Paul Feinman was appointed as the New York Court of Appeals' first out homosexual judge. As

Serbia's first openly homosexual (and first female) prime minister, Ana Brnabi made history by being the region's first head of state to participate in an LGBT pride march, which she did in Belgrade. As the first openly gay (and first female) co-chair of Alternative for Germany, Alice Weidel was also elected to the Federal Diet of Germany. As the first transgender lawmaker in Virginia, Danica Roem was elected. When Andrea Jenkins won a seat on the Minneapolis City Council, she made history as the nation's first openly transgender black woman to hold elective office. When Tyler Titus, a transgender man, won a seat on the Erie School Board, he made history by being the first openly transgender person elected to public office in Pennsylvania. He and Phillipe Cunningham were the first openly trans males to be elected to public office in the United States when they were both elected to the Minneapolis City Council on the same night. The first openly gay legislator in Oklahoma was Allison Ikley-Freeman. Palm Springs elected the country's first all-LGBT municipal council, which included three gay men, a transgender woman, and a bisexual woman. By legally removing transgender identities from its list of disorders related to mental health, Denmark became the second country to do so. The General Assembly of the Unitarian Universalist Association agreed to replace the terms "men and women" with the word "people" in the interest of providing inclusive terminology for non-binary, genderqueer, gender fluid, agender, intersex, two-spirit, and polygender individuals. The second source of faith among the six sources of the living tradition now includes "Words and deeds of prophetic people which challenge us to confront powers and structures of evil with justice, compassion, and the transforming power of love," as stated in the denomination's bylaws. The first former professional cyclist to publicly transition was Philippa York, formerly known as Robert Millar, after coming out as transgender. The first openly transgender *Playboy* Playmate was Ines Rau. For the first time, the US Military Health Agency granted funding for sex reassignment surgery for a U.S. military serviceman who was currently on active duty. A course of treatment for gender reassignment had already been started for the patient, an army soldier who identified as a woman. The treatment, which the attending physician determined to be medically essential, was carried out on November 14 in a private hospital because U.S. military facilities lacked the appropriate surgical experience. The first youth facility in the United Kingdom focused solely on LGBTQ+ young people was launched in Melton Mowbray, Leicestershire. On 21 January, LGBT Melton was established, and on 6 March, it held its official grand opening. Anthony Marvin, who founded LGBT Melton, was given the Leicester Pride Unsung Hero Award in recognition of his work and support for the LGBTQ+ community. Rutland and the rest of Leicestershire were now included in the services offered by LGBT Melton. The "Asexuality in Arabic" social media groups were established in 2017 by Nabil Allal and A'laa Yasin. Sarah Costello and Kayla Kaszyca began hosting the podcast *Sounds Fake But Okay*. Kaszyca "identifies as demisexual and straight," while Costello "identifies as aro ace."

In **2018**, same-sex marriage laws were passed in Jersey, Alderney, Bermuda (after the Supreme Court decision), and Costa Rica (to take effect by 26 May 2020). Trinidad and Tobago, India decriminalized homosexuality. Theresa May, the prime minister of the United Kingdom, apologized and expressed "deep remorse" for Britain's part in enforcing colonial laws that criminalized LGBT persons throughout the Commonwealth and the legacy of violence and prejudice that persists to this day. 36 of the 53 Commonwealth nations still had criminalization legislation in place when the apology was made. The first openly homosexual collegiate football player to score a touchdown was Wyatt Pertuset. Male competitors who were openly homosexual competed in the Winter Olympics for the first time ever this year. The tallest mountain on each continent according to both the Messner and Bass lists, Silvia Vasquez-Lavado completed the Seven Summits and became the first openly homosexual woman to do so. The first Pride celebration in Antarctica was conducted on June 9 in a bar in McMurdo Station in the Ross Dependency by 30 to 40 researchers, 12 of whom identified as LGBT. Stav Strashko made history by being the first openly transgender actress to be nominated for a Best Actress Ophir Award. After being ordained, Sandra Lawson became the first openly homosexual, black, female rabbi in history. Adam Rippon became the first out homosexual athlete from the United States to ever make it to the Winter Olympics. He became the first out homosexual American athlete to earn a medal at the Winter Olympics when, that year, he took home a bronze medal for the United States in the figure skating team competition. Jessica Platt, a player in the Canadian Women's Hockey League, became the first transgender person in North American professional hockey to come out. At West Point, Vinny Franchino and Daniel Hall wed to become the first active-duty, same-sex couple. *Strong Island*, which was both produced and directed by Yance Ford, received an *Academy Award* nomination for Best Documentary Feature. As a result, Ford was both the first openly transgender filmmaker and the first openly transgender male to get an *Academy Award* nomination. Laverne Cox made history by becoming the first openly transgender person to grace the cover of a *Cosmopolitan* publication, especially the February 2018 edition of *Cosmopolitan South Africa*. The first openly transgender lady to be featured in *British Vogue* was Paris Lees. The first openly homosexual K-pop artist, Holland, released his first single, *Neverland*. For their work on *Mudbound*, Dee Rees and Virgil Williams were nominated for an Oscar Award for Best Adapted Screenplay, making Rees the first LGBT black woman and lesbian to be nominated in any literary category. Because she was a lesbian, Rachel Morrison also made history as the first lesbian to be nominated for an Oscar Award for Best Cinematography. The first openly homosexual man to win a gold medal at any Winter Olympics was Canadian Eric Radford. Bishop Juan Cardona blessed Jhon Botia Miranda to serve as a pastor, making him the first openly homosexual pastor to be consecrated in the Methodist Church of Colombia and all of Latin America. As the first movie ever made by a major studio to center on a gay teen relationship, *Love, Simon* was released. Todd Harrity became the first out homosexual professional male squash player in the world when he came out as gay. At UFC 224 on May 12, 2018, Raquel Pennington and Amanda Nunes squared off for the UFC Women's Bantamweight Championship. By technical knockout in the fifth round, Pennington was defeated. This was the first UFC event to feature two openly homosexual combatants in the main event. The LGBT acronym was first used by the Vatican in a formal declaration. The first same-sex couple to grace the cover of *ESPN's Body Issue* was Sue Bird and Megan Rapinoe. The first openly homosexual major general in the Israel Defense Forces was Sharon Afek. Beth Ford became the first out homosexual woman to lead a *Fortune 500* firm when she was chosen CEO of Land O'Lakes. In the United States, no football player has ever played for a military institution before Bradley Kim of the Air Force Academy came out as homosexual. Mike Jacobs came out as bisexual, becoming the nation's first sitting judge to do so. A bill designating the LGBTQ Veterans Memorial in Desert Memorial Park as California's official LGBTQ veterans memorial was signed into law. As a result, California became the first state in the US to formally recognize LGBTQ veterans of the armed forces. The first male professional golfer to openly come out as homosexual was Tadd Fujikawa, who did so in a post on Instagram. Producing *Strong Island* earned Yance Ford and Joslyn Barnes an Emmy for Exceptional Merit in Documentary Filmmaking, making Ford the first openly transgender person, the first openly transgender man, and the first openly transgender person of color to win a Creative Arts Emmy. On September 22, 2018, Lord Ivar Mountbatten wed James Coyle, his same-sex partner, becoming the first member of the British monarch's extended family to do so. In West Hollywood, the nation's first citywide Bi Pride celebration took place. Patricio Manuel made history by becoming the first openly transgender man to compete in professional boxing in the United States. He also made history by becoming the first openly transgender man to triumph in a pro boxing match. *The Prom* cast members participated in Macy's Thanksgiving Day Parade, and they concluded their performance with the parade's first same-sex kiss. The first openly transgender model to participate in a Calvin Klein fashion show was Ariel Nicholson. The first prime minister of New Zealand to march in an LGBT pride parade was Jacinda Ardern. Kevin de León was replaced as Senate President Pro Tempore by Toni Atkins. As a result, she became the first openly lesbian and female leader of the California State Senate. When the Democrats nominated Christine Hallquist for governor of Vermont, she made political history by becoming the country's first openly transgender nominee for governor. Mike Jacobs came out as bisexual, becoming the nation's first sitting judge to do so. As a candidate for the U.S. Senate, Kyrsten Sinema made history by being the first openly bisexual person to get a major party nomination. Kyrsten Sinema was elected to the U.S. Senate as the first openly bisexual person. Graça Fonseca became the country of Portugal's first openly homosexual minister. As the first openly homosexual prime minister to win a second term, Xavier Bettel made history. As the first openly homosexual deputy prime minister to win a second term, Etienne Schneider made history. As the first openly homosexual person to be elected governor of a US state, Jared Polis won the election for governor of Colorado. He wasn't the first homosexual governor, either; on August 12, 2004, Jim McGreevey, the 52nd governor of New Jersey, came out as gay after winning the position but resigned during his term. The first openly LGBT person to be elected governor in the US was bisexual Kate Brown, who was elected as Oregon's governor in 2016. Sharice Davids was elected as the first openly LGBTQ member of the Kansas congressional delegation, the first out homosexual person to represent Kansas at the federal level, and the first Native American woman to serve in the US House. Angie Craig became the first openly lesbian mother and the first openly homosexual person from Minnesota to be elected to the US Congress. The first openly homosexual Muslim to be elected to politics in the United States was Ahmad Zahra, who was chosen to serve on the Fullerton city council. Chris Pappas was elected as New Hampshire's first openly homosexual representative to Congress. The first openly bisexual and first openly gay woman elected to Congress from California is Katie Hill. The first openly homosexual person to hold a statewide office in California's history, Ricardo Lara, was elected as the state's insurance commissioner. The first openly LGBTQ person to be elected to the state legislature of Nebraska was Megan Hunt, who was openly bisexual. On June 29, 2018, Angela Ponce became the first openly transgender contestant for *Miss Universe* and became the first openly transgender woman to be named Miss Spain. The first documented instance of a transgender woman nursing was described by *Transgender Health* as occurring in the United States with a transgender woman who nursed her adoptive child. Jessica Platt, a player in the Canadian Women's Hockey League, became the first transgender person in North American professional hockey to come out. The first openly transgender presenter at the *Academy Awards* in history was Daniela Vega. 2018 saw the debut of Pakistani television's first openly transgender newsreader, Marvia Malik. In The Go-Go's-inspired musical *Head Over Heels*, Peppermint made her Broadway debut. While performing the part of Pythio, Peppermint made history by becoming the first trans woman to create a lead character on Broadway, which took place between 23 June 2018 and 26 July. When the Democrats nominated Christine Hallquist for governor of Vermont, she made political history by being the first openly transgender candidate for governor to get support from a significant political party in the United States. Patricio Manuel made history by becoming the first openly transgender man to compete in professional boxing in the United States. He also made history by becoming the first openly transgender man to triumph in a pro boxing match. In 2018, Colombia prosecuted the murder of a transgender woman as femicide for the first time, sentencing Davinson Stiven Erazo Sánchez to 20 years in a mental institution for "aggravated femicide" a year after he had murdered Anyela Ramos Claros. On the TV Land series *Younger*, Jesse James Keitel portrayed the first non-binary character. 2018 saw the release of I Don't Want Sex, an episode of the BBC Three series *The Sex Map of Britain* that focused on asexuality.

In **2019**, same-sex marriage laws were passed in Austria, Taiwan (first in Asia), the Mexican states of San Luis Potosí, Hidalgo, Baja California Sur, Nuevo León and Aguascalientes, and Ecuador. Civil union laws were introduced in San Marino, Monaco, and the Cayman Islands. Angola and Botswana decriminalized homosexuality. Anti-discrimination laws were enacted in San Marino (constitutional amendment). The first out homosexual Democratic presidential candidate in American history and the first to participate in a nationally broadcast presidential debate was Pete Buttigieg. The first openly transgender members of the US military to publicly testify before Congress were Army Capt. Alivia Stehlik, Navy Lt. Cmdr. Blake Dremann, Army Capt. Jennifer Peace, Army Staff Sgt. Patricia King, and Navy Petty Officer 3rd Class Akira Wyatt. Lori Lightfoot became the first openly LGBT mayor of Chicago, Illinois on April 2, 2019. The first openly homosexual mayor of Madison, Wisconsin, was Satya Rhodes-Conway. As Tampa, Florida's first openly homosexual mayor, Jane Castor won the election. Nathan Ivie, a commissioner for Utah County, came out as homosexual, making him the state's first out gay Republican official. President Trump tweeted his recognition of LGBT Pride Month, making him the first Republican president to do so. During LGBT Pride Month, the governors of New York, Michigan, Wisconsin, Colorado, and California, for the first time raised the LGBT pride flag from their state capitols or executive mansions. During Trans Day of Remembrance in November 2019, transgender community activist Lauren Pulido flew the transgender pride flag over the California state capitol. This was apparently the first time the flag had been raised over a state legislative building in the country. Mounir Baatour, a lawyer and LGBT activist, entered the race for president of Tunisia in 2019 as the first openly homosexual man to do so in the Arab world. Ana Brnabić, the prime minister of Serbia, is said to be the first prime minister in a same-sex relationship whose partner gave birth while the prime minister was in office. Brnabi's spouse, Milica Đurđić, gave birth to a son. Gianmarco Negri became Italy's first openly transgender mayor when he was chosen to serve as mayor of Tromello. The first Head of State to address a EuroPride march was Alexander Van der Bellen, the president of Austria, in June 2019. Iris Eliisa Rauskala, Minister of Education, Science, and Research, became Austria's first openly LGBT minister in June when she came out as a lesbian and revealed she was married to a woman. Being the first openly homosexual minister in the Israeli cabinet, Amir Ohana made history. Meretz became the first Israeli party to elect an openly homosexual person as its head when Nitzan Horowitz defeated incumbent Tamar Zandberg in a leadership challenge. Jim Watson made the announcement that he was coming out as homosexual on August 17, 2019, in an opinion piece for the Ottawa Citizen, making history as the city's first openly gay mayor. Taiga

Ishikawa became the first openly homosexual man to be elected to either chamber of the National Diet when he won the 2019 Japanese House of Councillors election. The British royal couple Prince Harry and Meghan Markle became the first royals known to observe LGBT Pride Month. In February 2019, Bernd Mönkebüscher became the first German Catholic priest to come out in public without problems, according to his bishop. The first Catholic priest in the Netherlands to come out publicly was Pierre Valkering. When *Ek Ladki Ko Dekha Toh Aisa Laga* was released, it was the first mainstream Bollywood movie to deal with a lesbian relationship. The first openly homosexual character to be shown in a Marvel Cinematic Universe film was co-director Joe Russo (credited as Gozie Agbo), who appeared in *Avengers: Endgame* as a man grieving the unexpected loss of a loved one. Becoming the first openly transgender performer of a main part in a typical opera in the US, German-born Lucia Lucas made her US debut as Don Giovanni with the *Tulsa Opera*. With the release of *Rocketman*, Paramount became the first significant Hollywood company to depict homosexual male intercourse on screen. In Jerusalem, under the supervision of Rabbi Daniel Landes, Daniel Atwood became the first openly homosexual Orthodox rabbi. *Under the Rainbow*, a documentary that primarily examines the life of Pamela Adie, an out Nigerian lesbian, was the first lesbian-focused film to be produced in Nigeria. Leyna Bloom made her feature film debut in *Port Authority* at the Cannes Film Festival, marking the first time in the festival's history that a trans woman of color had a major role. The first openly transgender woman of color to land a deal with a major multimedia firm was Janet Mock, who secured a three-year deal with Netflix granting them exclusive rights to her TV series and a first-look option on feature film ideas. The first LGBT pride march was organized in North Macedonia. On September 9, 2019, Sarajevo, the nation's capital, hosted Bosnia and Herzegovina's first pride celebration. In the episode "The Last Crusade," which featured a lesbian pair named Aunt Holiday and Auntie Lofty, the Discovery Family animated series *My Little Pony* included a same-sex relationship for the first time. Broadway's first-known onstage same-sex marriage took place on that stage following a performance of *The Prom* at the Longacre Theatre on Broadway. It was a marriage between two women. *El corazón nunca se equivoca* (The Heart is Never Wrong), a primetime telenovela hosted by homosexual men, debuted on Univision. The first homosexual wedding featured on *Songs of Praise* was that of Jamie Wallace and Ian McDowall at Glasgow's Rutherglen United Reformed Church. The first artist to come out as gay while having a number-one single was Lil Nas X. Later when the Country Music Association Awards were announced, he was the first out homosexual male to receive a nomination. The first publicly homosexual gospel singer from Rwanda was Albert Nabonibo, who came out as gay. Billy Porter became the first out homosexual black male to be nominated and win in any lead acting category at the Primetime Emmys when he was nominated for and went on to win the award for Best Lead Actor in a Drama Series for the television series *Pose*. On September 16, 2019, Lilly Singh debuted *A Little Late with Lilly Singh*, making her the first late-night host to ever openly identify as bisexual. The National Board of Directors of Planned Parenthood welcomed Meghan Stabler as the organization's first openly transgender member. The editors of *The Advocate* magazine selected Meghan as one of their 2019 Champions of Pride. Indya

Moore made history by being the first openly transgender person to appear on the cover of *Elle* magazine in the United States. Zach Barak, who portrayed Peter Parker's classmate in *Spider-Man: Far From Home*, made history by being the first openly transgender actor in the Marvel Cinematic Universe. Laverne Cox was the first openly transgender woman to appear on the cover of *British Vogue* when Meghan, Duchess of Sussex, the magazine's guest editor, selected her as one of fifteen people to represent the September 2019 edition. In August 2019, Victoria's Secret hired Valentina Sampaio as their first openly transgender model. During the *Imagen Awards*, MJ Rodriguez made history by being the first openly transgender woman to win Best Actress - Television. The first openly transgender model to be hired by Chanel was Teddy Quinlivan. The first openly transgender person to moderate a presidential discussion in the United States was Angelica Ross. The first range of gender-neutral dolls was introduced by Mattel and was called Creatable World. The first openly lesbian lady to participate in the *Miss Universe* pageant was Swe Zin Htet. While she participated in *Miss Universe* 2013, Patricia Yurena Rodriguez of Spain waited until after the event to announce her identity. The first Trans Pride march in London took place. As the first out homosexual woman, Megan Rapinoe made history in the annual *Sports Illustrated* swimsuit issue. The first male soccer player from Australia to come out as homosexual was Andy Brennan. The first sportsperson from India to officially admit being in a same-sex relationship was Dutee Chand. When Nyla Rose joined All Elite Wrestling (AEW), she made history as the first openly transgender person to join a significant American professional wrestling organization. In Wimbledon, Alison van Uytvanck and

Greet Minnen, both from Belgium, made history as the first openly gay doubles team. As a member of the University of Montana women's team, June Eastwood became the first openly transgender athlete to participate in NCAA Division I cross country. When Amanda Sauer-Cook served as a center judge for the Alliance of American Football, she made history by being the first openly homosexual referee to work in a significant professional football league. Emi Salida, a British YouTuber who identified as asexual, was featured alongside Yasmin Benoit in a Sky News program about asexuality when she was 18 years old. The first openly asexual character on the British soap series *Emmerdale* was Liv Flaherty, played by actress Isobel Steele. Elizabeth Hopkinson, a romantic asexual novelist from Bradford, England, started recreating traditional fairy tales with asexual twists. For Pride in London in 2019, Yasmin Benoit presented the city's first bar with an asexual theme. Yasmin Benoit made history by being the first openly asexual woman to be featured on the cover of a UK magazine in an edition of *Attitude* headlined "The Activists". Washington became the first state in the union to celebrate Asexual Awareness Week, and Jay Inslee, the governor, signed a ceremonial proclamation on the occasion.

In **2020**, same-sex marriage laws were passed in Northern Ireland, Costa Rica, Sark, and the Mexican state of Tlaxcala. Nevada became the first U.S. state to constitutionally protect same-sex marriage. Civil union laws were enacted in Monaco, Cayman Islands and Montenegro. Homosexuality was no longer a criminal offence in Gabon. Anti-discrimination laws were adopted in the United States (Supreme Court Ruling), Switzerland, Barbados, North Macedonia, and the Marshall Islands. The first openly homosexual candidate to win a presidential primary or caucus in the United States was Pete Buttigieg. Richard Grenell was the first openly homosexual person to hold a cabinet-level job in the United States when he temporarily served as interim director of national intelligence under the Trump administration. Peyton Rose Michelle Theriot, the first openly transgender woman elected to a political post in the state of Louisiana, won the election for the female seat on the Democratic State Central Committee for the 46th District (seat A), representing St. Martin, Iberia, and St. Landry. Karine Jean-Pierre held the position of vice presidential chief of staff for the first time as an out homosexual woman. As the first openly gay woman elected to the Raleigh City Council, Stormie Forte made history. Sam Park, Robert Garcia, and Malcolm Kenyatta made history by being the first openly gay keynote speakers at a Democratic National Convention. Sarah McBride was elected as the nation's first transgender state senator. The first openly homosexual black males to be elected to Congress were Mondaire Jones and Ritchie Torres. Torres became the first openly gay Afro Hispanic elected to Congress as a result of this. The first transgender person to be elected to the Vermont General Assembly was Taylor Small. The United States' first elected non-binary state lawmaker is Mauree Turner. Stephanie Byers, a member of the Chickasaw Nation and the first Native American transgender person elected to politics in the United States, was elected to the Kansas state House of Representatives. She became the first transgender person to be elected to the Kansas state legislature as a result of this election. The transgender community was mentioned for the first time by the president-elect Joe Biden in his victory address. As mayor of Palm Springs, California, Christy

Holstege made history as the first openly bisexual mayor in the United States. Alex Lee became the first openly bisexual member of the California State Assembly. The Speaker of the Maine House of Representatives, Ryan Fecteau, became the first openly homosexual person to hold that position. Sean Patrick Maloney was chosen as the Democratic Congressional Campaign Committee's chairman for the first time as an out homosexual person. The first openly homosexual justice of the California Supreme Court, Martin Jenkins, was sworn in. As the first openly homosexual mayor of San Diego, Todd Gloria was elected. Pete Buttigieg became the first openly out homosexual cabinet nominee in American history when President Joe Biden announced him as his choice for the position of Secretary of Transportation. David Ortiz was the first openly bisexual person to be elected as a lawmaker in Colorado. Layla Moran, a UK lawmaker, came out as pansexual in an interview, making her the first lawmaker in the country to do so. Petra De Sutter, the first transgender deputy prime minister in Europe and the most senior trans politician in the continent, was sworn in as one of the seven deputy prime ministers in the administration of Belgian Prime Minister Alexander De Croo. The first professional rugby union player to come out as bisexual while still playing was Levi Davis, who came out as bisexual. At a Super Bowl, Katie Sowers made history as the first openly female and homosexual offensive assistant. Curdin Orlik became the first openly homosexual male professional athlete in Swiss sports as well as the first Schwingen athlete to come out as gay. Sebastian Vega became Argentina's first openly gay professional basketball player when he came out as homosexual. Chris Mosier made history by being the first openly transgender male athlete to ever compete in an Olympic trial with other males; however, he was injured and was unable to complete the race. Megan Youngren made history by being the first openly transgender athlete in American history to compete at the Olympic marathon trials. First openly lesbian to win the UCI Downhill Mountain Bike World Championship was Camille Balanche. Mara Gómez became the first transgender football player to compete in an Argentine league's top division. Soleil "Ewok" Wheeler of FaZe Clan came out as transgender, making him the first transgender man to play for a T1 esports team. Devin Ibanez, an American rugby player, became the first openly homosexual player in Major League Rugby after coming out. Nyla Rose, the first openly transgender woman to win a world title in a significant American wrestling organization, won the AEW Women's World Championship on Dynamite. The first Disney and Pixar short with a gay main character and plot was released, and it was titled *Out*. Disney's first animated canonically LGBT+ female regular characters were Luz Noceda and Amity Blight from *The Owl House*. *The Christmas Home* made its debut, becoming the first Hallmark film to prominently feature a same-sex relationship. *The Christmas Setup* was the first LGBTQ-themed Christmas movie that Lifetime has ever shown. Jesse James Keitel became the first nonbinary actor to portray a nonbinary series regular on primetime television when *Big Sky* debuted. The first character in an all-ages animated series to explicitly come out as homosexual was Benson from *Kipo and the Age of Wonderbeasts*. As Argentina's first openly transgender newscaster, Diana Zurco made history. At the Sao Paulo Carnival parade, Camila Prins made history as the first openly transgender woman to command the drum line of a prestigious samba school. The first openly transgender model for the *Sports Illustrated* Swimsuit Issue was Valentina Sampaio in 2020. The first openly bisexual candidate to compete for the Miss USA crown was Rachel Slawson. The first LGBTQ marching band to take the stage in the Macy's Thanksgiving Day Parade was the Lesbian and Gay Big Apple Corps. In the year 2020, the allosexual woman Jaymee Mak co-wrote, co-produced, and co-starred in the short movie *It's Not You. It's Not Me.*, inspired by her relationship with an asexual man. Jaymie Doyle served as the host of the inaugural Virtual Asexual Pride, which ran from June 17 to June 30. Asexual Pride for Ireland and Northern Ireland was meant to be continued digitally through the Virtual Asexual Pride, which was staged online via social media in response to the COVID-19 pandemic.

In **2021**, same-sex marriage laws were passed in Chile comes into effect March 2022), Switzerland (to come into effect in July 2022), the Mexican states of Baja California (codification), Sonora, Sinaloa, Querétaro, Guanajuato (by government decree), Zacatecas and Yucatan. Bhutan decriminalized homosexuality. Anti-discrimination laws came into effect in Angola (protections with regard to sexual orientations for employment, discrimination and hate crimes), Namibia (court ruling), and Botswana (2019 court ruling upheld by Supreme Court). At the Capital Pride Walk in Washington, D.C., Kamala Harris made history by becoming the first vice president of the United States to participate while still in office. In July 2021, Eduardo Leite came out, becoming Brazil's first openly homosexual governor. The first openly homosexual person to hold a cabinet position in the Greek government was Nicholas Yatromanolakis. Pete Buttigieg became the first openly homosexual person to be confirmed by the Senate to a Cabinet position as well as the first non-acting openly gay member of the United States Cabinet. Aung Myo Min became the country of Myanmar's first openly homosexual cabinet minister. As President of the Reykjavk City Council, Alexandra Briem became the first openly transgender political officeholder in Iceland. On *RuPaul's Drag Race*, Gottmik made history as the first openly transgender male competitor. First openly transgender news anchor in Bangladesh is Tashnuva Anan Shishir. Elliot Page made history by being the first openly transgender man to grace the cover of *Time*. TJ Osborne became the first openly homosexual singer signed to a significant country music company when he came out as gay on February 3, 2021. When Patti Harrison voiced the minor role of Tail Chief in *Raya and the Last Dragon*, she made history as the first transgender performer to be recognized in a Disney animated picture. The U.S. Senate officially approved Rachel Levine on March 24 to be the country's assistant secretary for health, making her the nation's first openly transgender official. The *Tasmanian Honour Roll of Women* honored Martine Delaney as the first openly transgender woman. The first US president to officially recognize the Transgender Day of Visibility was Joe Biden. Adrian Hanstock became the first openly homosexual police leader of a British police force when he was appointed as the interim Chief Constable of the British Transport Police. The United States' first openly transgender Black woman elected to a public school board was Alana Gisele Banks. The magazine *The Knot* featured the first openly homosexual couple, Jonathan Bennett and Jaymes Vaughan. The Evangelical Lutheran Church of America installed Megan Rohrer as a bishop, making her the first openly transgender and non-binary bishop in any Christian church. The first same-sex dancing couple appeared on the American edition of *Dancing with the Stars*. The first governor to recognize Bisexual Pride Day in the United States was Tom Wolf, governor of Pennsylvania. In the *Wonder Woman* series of DC Comics, Bia made her debut as the first out transgender Amazon. The first openly transgender person to appear on the *Vogue* cover was Ariel Nicholson. On April 14, 2021, Colton Underwood came out as homosexual, becoming him the first openly gay *Bachelor* lead in the history of the show. In addition, following Michael Sam, he was the second openly homosexual NFL free agent to come out. On June 21, 2021, Carl Nassib came out as homosexual, becoming the first openly gay player in the NFL. Luke Prokop, a Canadian who was selected by the Nashville Predators in the 2020 NHL Entry Draft, made history by coming out as homosexual and signing a contract with a National Hockey League team.

In **2022**, same-sex marriage laws were passed in Slovenia (July 2022 in effect, October 2022 codification), Cuba (referendum), Mexico (Nationwide, following legalization in the states of Durango, Guerrero, Mexico, Tabasco, Tamaulipas, Veracruz and Yucatán), Chile, Switzerland and Andorra. In the United States, same-sex marriages were codified via the *Respect for Marriage Act*. Antigua & Barbuda, Saint Kitts and Nevis, Singapore and Barbados decriminalized homosexuality. Anti-discrimination laws were adopted in Spain and Nevada. Nevada became the first US state in history to accept the addition of the phrases "sexual orientation and gender identity or expression" to its state-based Constitution when voters approved Question 1 by a margin of 58% in November 2022. Jowelle de Souza became the first openly transgender senator in the Caribbean. She represented Trinidad and Tobago. After coming out, Jamie Wallis became the first openly transgender member of the UK House of Commons. The first openly lesbian White House press secretary was Karine Jean-Pierre. At the Capital Pride Festival in Washington, D.C., Kamala Harris made history by becoming the first vice president of the United States to speak while in office. She also hosted the first LGBTQ+ Pride Month celebration held at the home of a vice president of the United States. Erika Hilton and Duda Salabert were the first openly transgender candidates to win seats in the Brazilian National Congress's Chamber of Deputies. George Santos was the first openly homosexual Republican elected to the U.S. Congress who was not an incumbent. The first openly homosexual candidate for Congress from Vermont was Becca Balint. The first openly transgender person to be elected to the Minnesota legislature was Leigh Finke. The first out LGBTQ women and first Black women elected to the Minnesota state Senate were Erin Maye Quade and Clare Oumou Verbeten. When James Roesener was chosen for Ward 8 in New Hampshire's 22nd state House District, he made history by being the first openly transgender male to be elected to any state legislature in the country. The first openly non-binary person elected to the Minnesota legislature was Alicia Kozlowski. The first openly non-binary person to be elected to the Montana legislature was SJ Howell. By being chosen as Speaker of the Knesset, Amir Ohana became the first openly LGBT person to hold that post in Israeli history. The first openly LGBTQ person to be elected to a public office in Louisiana was Davante Lewis. The first openly homosexual black person to be elected to the state legislature of California was Corey Jackson. The first publicly homosexual governor of Massachusetts and the first openly lesbian governor of the United States was

Maura Healey. The first openly homosexual man from Illinois to be elected to Congress was Eric Sorensen. Erick Russell was chosen to serve as Connecticut's state treasurer, making him the country's first out homosexual African American elected to a statewide position. Jolanda Jones was elected to the Texas state senate as the first openly homosexual black person. It wasn't until the general election of 2022 that openly Gay candidates could be found in every state of the Union. In the United States, Willow Pill made history by being the first openly transgender contestant to win a normal season of *RuPaul's Drag Race*. The role of Thought 1 in the musical *A Strange Loop* earned L. Morgan Lee a nomination for Best Performance by a Featured Actress in a Musical, making her the first openly transgender person to get a Tony Award nomination in an acting category. Ariana DeBose, who played Anita in the Steven Spielberg-directed 2021 adaptation of *West Side Story*, made history by being the first LGBT woman of color and Afro-Latina to win an Oscar for acting. In the episode "Families," Penny Polar Bear's mums served as the first representation of a same-sex relationship on *Peppa Pig*. The film *Bros* was released and it was the first homosexual romantic comedy produced by a major studio with an all LGBTQ main cast. Molly Kearney was introduced as the first out non-binary cast member of *Saturday Night Live* in September 2022. Sam Smith became the first openly non-binary person to top the Billboard Hot 100 with the song *Unholy*, while Kim Petras became the first openly transgender woman to accomplish this with the same song. Amy Schneider was the first openly transgender contestant to get to the *Jeopardy!* Tournament of Champions finals and claim victory. The openly homosexual main character in the movie *Strange World* marked the debut of the first openly LGBTQ major character created by Walt Disney Animation Studios. *The Holiday Sitter*, the first Christmas movie with an LGBTQ lead on Hallmark Channel, debuted. As Vice President of Legal and Business Affairs at Venice Music, transgender man Dani Oliva made history as the first openly transgender executive at a significant music label. On January 15, 2022, Carl Nassib played in an NFL playoff game as the league's first out gay player. Lia Thomas, a swimmer, won the women's 500-yard freestyle with a time of 4:33.24 to become the first openly transgender athlete to win an NCAA Division I national championship in any sport. When Ryan Resch came out while working for the Phoenix Suns, he became the first openly homosexual person in NBA front office history to supervise basketball operations. Igor Benevenuto made history by coming out as gay as the first FIFA-ranked soccer referee. The first Irish men's international hockey player to come out as homosexual was Peter Caruth. The first openly homosexual member of the Russian national team was Nadezhda Karpova. Travis Shumake made history as the first openly homosexual racer to take the track at a major National Hot Rod Association race. The first Olympian to come out as a trans man was Ellia Green. When Jamie Hunter won the U.S. Women's Open, she made history by being the first openly transgender snooker player to achieve that feat. The first senior male soccer player in Scotland to come out as gay was Zander Murray. The first openly gay wrestler to win an All Elite Wrestling championship was Anthony Bowens. Lucas Krzikalla came out as gay, becoming the first active male athlete in a professional team sport in Germany and the first openly gay player in the Handball-Bundesliga. The first openly gay football player at a historically black college or university was Byron Perkins of Hampton University. When Isaac Humphries came out as gay, he became the first male basketball player from Australia and the first openly gay player in the National Basketball League. When Justine Lindsay joined the Carolina TopCats, she made history as the first openly transgender individual to join a National Football League cheerleading squad. The first openly homosexual male wrestler to join with Impact Wrestling was Jai Vidal. The Los Angeles Fire Department's first openly gay and female chief was Kristin Crowley. The first openly gay president of the American Psychiatric Association was Petros Levounis. Therese Stewart was confirmed as the first openly lesbian chief justice of a California appellate court; more precisely, she was approved as chief justice of Division Two of the 1st District Court of Appeal. The Supreme Court of India gave LGBTQ people family and cohabitation rights on par with those of married couples in August 2022.

Despite all of this celebration of our existence, numerous nations are experiencing regression. In the following chapter, we'll take a closer look at some of the disturbing events that took place in 2023.

CHAPTER FOUR

THE OPPRESSION SEEMS TO LINGER ON

Despite the fact that we are in the twenty-first century, the outside world still views our community with disdain. Our digital devices constantly bear news about statements made by eminent personalities and laws being passed throughout the world that are an assault on our community. From being imprisoned for merely identifying as LGBTQIA+ to restrictions on drag events and gender-affirming healthcare for transgender children, our generation is witnessing overwhelming regression in human rights across the world.

A public statement against marriage equality rights in India was made by 21 former judges in the form of the open letter that appears below. The open letter was signed by 21 individuals, including former Chief Justice of Rajasthan High Court Justice (retired) S. N. Jha, Justice (retd) M. M. Kumar, former Chief Justice of Jammu and Kashmir High Court, Gujarat Lokayukta Justice (retd) S. M. Soni and Justice (retd) S. N. Dhingra.

"We are a group of former Judges, the conscientious and concerned citizens of India, having been exasperated and agonised over the continuous onslaught against the basic tenets of Bharatiya marriage Traditions and Family System by vested interest groups, write to you to draw your kind attention towards one such issue - legalisation of same-sex marriage. The issue is being considered by the Supreme Court and has gained momentum in recent past in the country consequent to it being referred to a Constitution Bench. The people of the nation, hailing from various strata of society across regional and religious lines, are deeply shocked by this western-tinted outlook that is being superimposed on Bharatiya society and culture to weaken the family system. Several jurists, thinkers, and intellectuals have expressed their serious concerns at its repercussions on the family, which is the basic unit of society.

The marriage as well as the family system in India is sui generis. In our humble opinion, legalising same-sex marriage will strike at the very root of the family system and thus will have devastating impact on the society at large. Marriage in India is a socio-religious sacramental union, not only between two individuals but between two families. It is evident since times immemorial, that the purpose of marriage is not confined only to the physical intimacy of partners but goes far beyond and is indispensable for the growth of society by way of procreation of progeny. Unfortunately, certain versed interest groups having no knowledge and regard of the civilizational importance of marriage have approached the Court praying for legalising of same-sex marriage. Any attempt at weakening a great and time- tested institution should be opposed vociferously by the society.

Indian cultural civilization has constantly been attacked for centuries but survived against all odds. Now in independent India it is facing attacks on its cultural roots by the superimposition of western thoughts, philosophies and practices which are not viable for this nation at all. The cancerous problems that the West is facing are sought to be imported into Bharat by vested interest groups through the misuse of judiciary as an institution in the name of right to choice.

While perusing the discourse on the issue of same sex marriage, it is pertinent to take lessons from the nations across the globe, specifically the American experience where as per its own official figures published by Centers for Disease Control and Prevention in the HIV Surveillance Report, for 2019 and 2020, it has been reported that 70% of new HIV-AIDS incidence in the country was amongst the gay and bisexual men. Therefore, legalising same-sex marriage might lead to an exponential rise in the number of HIV-affected. Giving priority to right to choice and personal liberty over right to life may cause severe consequences in the future.

In addition to the health consequences amongst the partners, there are studies to state that legalising homosexual marriage will have negative consequences over the children adopted by such couples, including their emotional and psychological development as well as on their nurturing in an environment and at the risk of significant population decline. Recognition of same sex marriage will change the entire gamut of all personal laws from marriage to adoption and succession. In the long run, there are serious concerns that the gene pool is also going to be weakened affecting the entire human race especially in terms of collective herd immunity and progressive evolution.

Therefore, owing to its devastating impact on children, family, and society, mindless attempts to ape the practices of West in India, especially by legalising same-sex marriage, would prove to be a death knell to the already crumbling family system and devastating impact on the society at large.

Since times immemorial, Bharat has a tradition of samvaad and shastrarth to inquire into the greater good for our society. Instead of having wide-range discussions and deliberations amongst the stakeholders and without there being any vociferous demand from any section of society, such a hasty judicial intervention is unfortunate, and totally unwarranted. The separation of powers is a part of the basic structure of the Indian Constitution. The exercise of law-making is an exclusive domain of the legislature and not the judiciary, especially in matters exclusively within social and political domain.

In view of the above, it is our concerted opinion that such sensitive Issue concerning the society at large be debated In the Parliament and State legislature as well. Even before bringing such kind of law, the opinion of the society must be obtained to ensure that the law must represent the wish of the society and do not fulfil the desire of few elite sections of the society.

We thus respectfully urge the conscious members of the society Including those who are pursuing the Issue of same-sex marriage In Supreme Court to refrain from doing so in the best Interest of Indian society and culture."

But here's the problem: they said a lot of things that were incorrect. First of all, apart from ignorant people who don't realize that there are numerous varieties of individuals, no one is "shocked" by the fundamental right to marriage equality. Neither homosexuality nor the LGBTQIA+ community "shocks" anyone. As I've previously explained in my earlier chapters, we have been around for several millennia, even in Indian culture. So no! There is no attempt to undermine the family structure by imposing a "western-tinted outlook" on Bharatiya society and culture. These 21 people have an obligation to educate themselves about our history and identity. They inhabit a fantasy universe in which cis-heteronormativity existed by itself. These individuals' conviction that "marriage in India is a socio-religious sacramental union, not only between two individuals but between two families," is acceptable. To each their own. They do not, however, have the authority to disregard the simple fact that people hold a wide range of beliefs. Not every person in the world, not just those in India, must share their values. How can we expect the well over 7 billion people on the planet, who represent various racial, ethnic, religious, and family origins, to share a single belief? How are we expected to all fit into such a tiny box? It is absurd to contemplate such an ideology at all. Secondly, contrary to the baseless argument regarding HIV/AIDS, legalizing same-sex marriages won't result in a rapid rise in the number of affected people. A National AIDS Control Organization (NACO) study found that heterosexual persons accounted for 83% of all HIV transmissions. Although LGBTQIA+ individuals are also at risk, using condoms or starting PrEP can help decrease transmission. Misconceptions in society are cultivated by the absence of sex education, coupled with the lack of HIV/AIDS education and dialogue. It would have made more sense if these 21 people had endorsed sex education rather than writing the aforementioned letter. Lastly, it's evident that they don't understand that no one is attempting to "turn the world gay" or whatever when they claim that studies show that legalizing homosexual marriages "will have negative consequences over the children adopted by such couples, including their emotional and psychological development as well as on their nurturing in an environment and at the risk of significant population decline". Hence, reproduction and progress will still be attainable in the world. If they genuinely cared about the future and children, they would work to get all of those orphans adopted. It is a fallacy to believe that "Indian cultural civilization has continuously been attacked for centuries but survived against all odds," since it is rather our vibrant community that has demonstrated resilience in the face of several attempts to eradicate us.

In opposition to the rights of LGBTQIA+ individuals who want to adopt, the National Commission for Protection of Child Rights (NCPCR) of India submitted an application to the Supreme Court with the argument that "Same-sex parents endanger their children's well-being". I do have to say that they have the audacity to bring up this point in their application, considering that cisgender heterosexual parents frequently contribute to the cause of children seeking adoption in the first place. In light of the fact that we would provide the numerous orphaned children with a loving home, it is ludicrous even to consider that LGBTQIA+ people would "endanger children" if they were parents. These people's views in this respect are not even surprising to me, and they happen to lose all sense of reasoning when they make such baseless remarks.

The LGBTQIA+ community encounters opposition from institutions that are meant to be the pillars of democracy not only in India but in other nations as well. Well over 400 anti-LGBTQIA+ laws have been introduced in the US over the past several months, as we have seen. Legislators have launched an assault on our beloved community—a community that merely seeks to live in peace, harmony, and happiness—by denying gender-affirming healthcare to transgender people, outlawing drag shows, and codifying prejudice into the law. It is absurd that these lawmakers are devoting their time and effort to alienating this non-threat demographic rather than focusing on gun reform. Considering that there have been so many mindless mass shootings in the US, legislation to control gun use should be drafted immediately. Uganda, an African nation, reinforced its laws against LGBTQIA+ people, with punishments ranging from fines and prison time to the death penalty. In a broadly circulated video, a member of the Ugandan parliament claims that the legislation is being introduced to maintain the morality of the nation. But what morals—disrespecting someone's existence, preventing someone from leading their own lives as they should, or torturing and killing people who are just existing like any other human being—was he referring to?

A large majority of Gulf nations, which are located east of the African continent, continue to maintain laws that prohibit homosexuality, and a few of them even enforce the death sentence on individuals who simply have consensual same-sex relationships. It breaks my heart to know that some of these nations make it so hard for LGBTQIA+ persons to even exit the country. Why should a person be forced to abide by someone else's tastes and preferences? In any case, to whom does life belong—to the individual or to society? One of the numerous problems to be held responsible for these negative sentiments about our community is colonization. It is clear from the earlier chapters that Europeans imposed harsh laws on the areas they colonized, especially those that related to the LGBTQIA+ community. But, even though we have, for the most part, moved past that terrible time period, its consequences still linger. People's mindsets have been misplaced, and we still have a lot of work to do before we can reap the rewards of equity.

I did some research to see where we are in terms of acceptability and whether or not we encounter prejudice. These are a few of the responses.

Katyayani, a 25-year-old intersex-to-transfemale Indian, believes that her country discriminates against LGBTQIA+ people despite the fact that her faith is accepting of people of any gender or sexual orientation. Even she is aware that we have always been valued and included in religion. I hope more people become aware of this reality. She highlights the significance of realizing that the freedom to feel comfortable in one's own skin is a matter of basic human rights. She maintains that on a crucial matter that needs equality and fairness, the majority cannot rule over the minority. How would you feel if society openly discriminated while the law mandated equality and non-discrimination? All the spaces previously occupied by women and the LGBT community have largely been taken over by cis-gender heterosexuals, mostly men. They are therefore afraid of receiving equal space and long-overdue considerations.

Yash, a 22-year-old bisexual Indian, feels that his nation is conservative and that talking about sex is prohibited. Often, people avoid discussing it in public. I think it preposterous that talking about sex is frowned upon in a nation that is essentially the birthplace of the Kama Sutra. If sexuality is forbidden, then aren't we all? Yash has gone through a lot of pain as a consequence of being bisexual. Most people seem to believe he is acting out or attempting to attract too much attention. He undoubtedly feels stifled in India because he lacks a feeling of self. He still thinks that India has a long way to go before accepting everyone, but more people are becoming aware of that anyway. Although I too think the LGBTQIA+ community will ultimately blend in, I don't think we should have to endure this much pain. When we were all intended to be on an equal footing, it is blatantly unjust. While he was in class 9, he had his first infatuation with a boy. That kid was quite polite, kind, and attractive. Yash used to blush whenever he spoke to him. His peers began to make fun of him and refer to him as "Gay" after noticing this behavior. For being gay, they would beat him, abuse him, and harass him. All of these shenanigans stopped when he tried to complain to his class coordinator about it.

Pratit, a 22-year-old queer Indian, believes that the community has many supporters and that we are treated fairly. He also thinks that everyone in our community ought to be treated fairly since, of all, we are all humans. He and I both concur on the latter. We must respect one another as fellow citizens in order to preserve the beauty of our town. I don't necessarily believe that our community is treated fairly, though. The so-called allies frequently treat us like a token. During the whole year, Pride Month is the only time we are given the impression that we are important.

An asexual person from India who wishes to remain anonymous believes that her community is not treated equitably. She has struggled with educating people about asexuality as well. One should undoubtedly educate themselves on the entire variety of identities that make up asexuality. It is intriguing to discover that, similar to how not everyone enjoys sweet treats, not everyone is attracted to people in the same manner.

The LGBTQIA+ community, according to Venicia, a 19-year-old bisexual Indian, is treated horribly. She adds by pointing out that we are perceived as a sin and a crime, that our rights don't appear to exist, that we are considered a failure to our families, and that even our existence is viewed as a mistake. Some individuals believe we are acting excessively because we seek attention. She feels that regardless of our identities, we simply want to be inclusive of everyone. She hasn't yet experienced any disrespect or harassment, but because she is openly bisexual, she occasionally runs into men who have a threesome fetish. She is sexually active and is sick of being invited to join them in bed or for threesomes. She detests the extreme fetishization of bisexual and lesbian women.

Raj, a 28-year-old demiromantic asexual from India, argues that how members of our community are treated varies depending on the culture since he occasionally notices that his group is treated differently by members of other cultures. A minority of individuals find it completely acceptable because it has been included in legendary myths, but the majority find it to be against culture. Moreover, he maintains that all identities are legitimate so long as they do not cause harm to or interfere with the lives of others. His theory that other cultures respond to our community differently is one with which I completely concur. Moreover, I believe that harmonious cultural fusion promotes a more open-minded perspective on a variety of subjects, including the LGBTQIA+ community. I believe we should all live in peace and refrain from meddling with others' lives. You don't have to become involved in someone's business if their identification makes you uncomfortable. That is their own unique individuality, after all. You should show respect for their existence if they are interested in involving you in that part of their life.

While there is still a lot of prejudice against LGBTQIA+ people, Glamika, an Indian woman in her late 20s, claims that attitudes have begun to change. They aren't just ordinary humans, in her opinion; they are also God's Children. She has dated more than a hundred heterosexual, handsome young men and has experienced more than a hundred breakups as a result of the denial of sexual relationships. She is now seeking out a suitable heteroromantic individual to spend the rest of her life with, and if she is unsuccessful, she will consider Lord Shree Krishna to be her soul mate.

According to Ron, a 70-year-old gay American, legal rights are dwindling at the federal level, thus rights and safety differ by state. He argues that in Christianity, love, not gender, sets the boundaries and that sex is a metaphor for the strength of God's love for us. According to him, since the community is as vast as the universe, any identities that respect oneself and others appear plausible. He also makes the point that mastering vocabulary, which leads to freedom, might be difficult for some of us.

According to Lightus, a 23-year-old asexual Indian, people from rural backgrounds are less accepting of the community and may not grasp the notion of alternative sexualities. Urban residents tend to be slightly more welcoming. He practices Roman Catholicism, which views homosexuality, bisexuality, and transgender people as sinners. Asexuality is not mentioned, despite the fact that it may be encouraged and associated with celibacy. Because of his emotional and aesthetic affinity to men, he formerly identified as gay. Yet as he aged, he gradually began to understand that he is asexual. He is aware that sexuality is a continuum and that some people may fall outside of one category and into one or many others. He claims that out of the LGBT+ community as a whole, the ace community is one of the rarest. He has also encountered prejudice from fellow LGBT+ people as someone who does not feel the necessity for sexual activity. Some gay/bi men have also linked asexuality to impotence. Choosing his identity can be challenging a lot of the time due to his emotional attraction. He often wonders if he identifies as gay or ace since he is emotionally and aesthetically drawn to men. The main reason he chooses to identify as an ace is that he values emotional connection over sexual closeness.

The treatment of LGBTQIA+ people, according to Rishabh, a 25-year-old non-binary individual from India, is problematic. As an adherent of Gagaism (ze is a fan of Lady Gaga), ze believes that love is love. Ze has witnessed that other LGBTQIA+ individuals can be pretty closed-minded and quite prejudiced against one another.

Veda, a 23-year-old bisexual from India, believes that LGBTQIA+ people do not receive fair treatment. There has been a significant transformation in India over the past several decades, where intellectuals and educated people are working together to raise awareness and combat discrimination, but there is still a long way to go. Over this period, a number of laws and regulations have developed in favor of gay people, including those that legalize the LGBTQ community, recognize live-in relationships as protected by the Constitution, and permit trans people to self-identify without undergoing surgery. Although these laws have undoubtedly improved the lives of LGBTQ+ people, a serious concern remains over their physical and mental security. However, unlike the judiciary, much of India has not made the same social strides. As a result, despite the passage of several laws, the country's social climate is still far from what I would consider ideal for gay people to live in. Although she is not a practicing Hindu, her family is. She was raised on tales of trans people playing significant parts in Apsara and Gandharva's pansexual genesis legends and complex "raasleela," or beginnings in heaven. She therefore never truly considered LGBT people to be sinister or ungodly beings. Hinduism was and is a fairly welcoming religion that strongly supports self-acceptance and selecting one's own path. She hasn't had much experience with religious trauma that is linked to her identity. The societal trauma was there for sure. She respects and is accepting of all gender identities and sexual orientations. Even if you don't agree with her position, it still stands. She has struggled a little with accepting her LGBT identity and communicating it to the people in her life. Because she is bisexual, which is sometimes connected with being "confused," others are less likely to recognize her orientation. As a result, "bi-erasure" is still a significant problem, even within the community. While on her journey, she intends to raise as much awareness as she can whilst also learning and developing from these experiences.

A 30-year-old gay person from India named Parijat claims that although LGBTQIA+ people are becoming more mainstream, society has not yet embraced them. He believes that his religion has responded positively as well. Only a select group of friends and college professors are aware of his sexual orientation. He continues by saying that everyone seems to have been quite encouraging, even his sister. She gave him a lift in terms of his sense of self.

A 21-year-old bisexual person from India alleges that, in her personal experience, most older people see the LGBTQIA+ community with disdain, apathy, and disgust. She has observed that individuals of her own age are far more welcoming of her. She thinks it is encouraging that individuals are making an effort to become better educated. Even though she doesn't practice any organized religion, she finds it very cool that some of Hinduism's deities are LGBTQIA+. She is unaware of what the relevant theological writings have to say about it, though. She doesn't actually discuss her sexuality all that often, but when she does, her mother reacts with contempt, so she avoids discussing personal experiences with her. But she has always been welcomed by her friends, and she is quite appreciative of them

The community experiences a lot of discrimination, according to Akshita, a 21-year-old bisexual woman from India, because not enough awareness is being offered to everyone. She does not relate her religious beliefs to her gender identity. She believes that everyone has the right to live their lives as they deem fit. Love is, after all, love.

Although not every member of the LGBTQIA+ community is completely free, Victorino, a 30-year-old gay man from India, contends that generally speaking, the manner in which they are treated is fair. Although the younger generation is rapidly becoming more tolerant in his opinion, certain religions are in fact not supportive of the community. He thinks that things are getting a little complicated because there are so many distinct identities being used. He also thinks that communities need to be more welcoming to greater opportunities. I have to add that since we have been around for millennia, it is evident from history just how massive our community is. It's not that "new" identities are appearing out of nowhere; rather, they are being acknowledged after enduring suppression from earlier generations, many of whom were LGBTQIA+ themselves.

A 25-year-old gay individual from India known as Mr. Galen argues that while things continue to be awful for those who identify as LGBTQIA+, they are steadily getting better. The majority of LGBTQIA+ identities, in his opinion, are "bullshit," while just a small minority are authentic. I have to disagree with that statement since everyone has complete validity in exactly how they identify. Since it is impossible for over seven billion human beings to identify in the same way as a single individual, there is no right or wrong approach, genuine identity, or genuine identity or fake identity, as I previously stated in this book. Galen adds, "We in the community say that people don't want to change, but the reality is that people in the community are so messed up. Therefore, we should accept ourselves before asking others to do so."

According to a 28-year-old gay Indian man who would like to stay anonymous various states treat LGBTQIA+ people differently. He is a Catholic, and many who follow his religion are very opposed to the LGBTQIA+ community. He adds by saying that in the same way that he is entitled to his identity, so are other LGBTQIA+ people.

The LGBTQIA+ community is subjected to persecution on a daily basis, according to a 28-year-old gay man from India named J. Ahmed. People are mocked and treated differently. His faith holds that homosexuality is a sin in the Muslim community. He feels that every person, regardless of sexual orientation or gender identity, deserves the same rights as everyone else. He advises young people who are struggling to pick just those they can trust to come out to and that it's normal to feel different.

Although being LGBTQIA+ is not criminally penalized in India, Shaswata, a 31-year-old gay man, reckons society persists in being far from embracing it. He has observed that daily episodes of assault, name-calling, mental torment, brutality, sexual misconduct, forced wedlock, etc. affect members of our community but go unreported. Transgender individuals are those who are most impacted. Despite being recognized legally, they face oppression as they seek out housing, employment, security, and other opportunities. He is a Bengali man with a Hindu upbringing, and he has never been taught to despise LGBTQIA+ individuals. He continues by saying that the Hijra people are revered in our society and that receiving their blessings is advantageous for both the child and the family. While there is no animosity, he adds, "We did, however, live in terror of them should they curse us". He supports the Ardhanariswar theory that purush (masculinity) and prakriti (femininity) can coexist in the same body. He makes an effort to be open to everyone, but there are occasions when he isn't particularly accommodating toward someone, and he subsequently regrets it. He tries to honestly perceive the individual and not what his mind has been trained to view, he adds. Everyone is free to be who they are and to want to achieve anything, which he supports. He has few friends from within the LGBTQIA+ community or in any other group because of his household and professional commitments. He claims to be a reclusive individual who takes a very long time to build relationships. He observes that many people befriend LGBTQIA+ individuals just to sexually or otherwise take advantage of them. He came across a few members of the community who harbored animosity toward the community and just enjoyed using sex to punish members of the community. Few of the people he met are actually decent people, and he is still friends with them.

According to an anonymous 28-year-old Indian asexual, "We (asexuals) are still viewed as outcasts in the community, but awareness is growing among the general public and there has been a slight change seen in the urban environment". Despite the fact that he is an atheist and does not practice his religion, Hinduism, regularly, he thinks that it does not reveal a lot about the community. He claims that being a part of the community is not a sin and is not condemned by the faith. It's as if we don't exist or are not to be mentioned, he continues. He notes that everything in the community revolves around cisgender homosexual or bisexual men. However, he points out that transgender black women are the reason why the community continues to thrive. Although there are no black people in the nation, he argues that the trans and hijra communities are vibrant. On whatever platform, the

Hijra community has not been effectively represented. "We see trans people working as lawyers and doctors, but they are trans, not hijras, and we need to ensure that hijras also have the same rights," he asserts. The word "community" as a whole bothers him personally. People boast that we are one, yet they subsequently attempt to downplay your identity or just bully you out. He states that he is an ace, has experienced medical concerns, and once encountered a cisgender homosexual man who described him as being "ugly as fuck." He is not bothered since he considers that as being truthful, but he disagrees when we state that we are a community. According to him, a community should uplift one another rather than denigrate members based on their size, color, race, health, appearance, or other characteristics.

LGBTQIA+ people are welcomed and seen as ordinary members of society, according to a 21-year-old gay man who resides in Germany. He argues that his faith is pro-LGBTQIA+, but sadly, other adherents of the same religion (Hinduism) do not share his views. He feels that everyone who is a part of the LGBTQIA+ community deserves to be accepted just as much as he does. He recently relocated, and one of the main reasons was so he could be himself without worrying about being persecuted. Moving away from family required some difficult choices, but he knows that it is for the best.

These distinct viewpoints show that although the world is advancing toward the sun, some people seem to be dragging us in the opposite direction. We undeniably have a "long way to go," as many of these participants have highlighted. How then can we continue to go in the direction of the light? This will be demonstrated in the next chapter.

CHAPTER FIVE

THE SOLUTION IS WALKING FORWARD TOGETHER

The LGBTQIA+ community has made considerable progress in recent years toward obtaining equal rights and legal protections. Yet, many LGBTQIA+ people throughout the world continue to experience prejudice, inequity, and violence. Both LGBTQIA+ and non-LGBTQIA+ people must band together in order to achieve the common objective of building a more inclusive and fair society in hopes of bringing about meaningful change. This chapter will examine why such unity is required, the potential obstacles, and methods that each of us as individuals may apply together to bring about positive change.

The campaign for LGBTQIA+ rights is a fight for justice and equality for all people, not just a minority group. When members of a minority group experience prejudice and persecution, it has a contagious effect on the entire society.

Those that identify as LGBTQIA+ are our friends, family, coworkers, and neighbors. The lives of individuals close to them are also impacted by discrimination against them. We can create a society that is more just and equitable for everyone if we work together.

However, the LGBTQIA+ community suffers particular difficulties that call for the activism and support of those who are not LGBTQIA+. LGBTQIA+ individuals have a greater tendency than their non-LGBTQIA+ counterparts to endure homelessness, poverty, and issues with their mental health. Discrimination, violence, and stigma against the LGBTQIA+ community are still pervasive. Non-LGBTQIA+ people may campaign for change, lobby for legislation that protects LGBTQIA+ rights, and support organizations that offer services and support to the LGBTQIA+ community by using their privilege and power.

When seeking to bring the LGBTQIA+ and non-LGBTQIA+ communities together, there may be a number of difficulties. Lack of awareness and education regarding LGBTQIA+ issues is one of the biggest obstacles. Those who are not LGBTQIA+ could not comprehend the difficulties and issues that LGBTQIA+ people endure, which could result in a lack of sympathy and support. LGBTQIA+ people, on the other hand, could be wary of non-LGBTQIA+ people or think that their experiences are not fully reflected or understood.

The existence of internal biases and prejudices among both societies presents another difficulty. LGBTQIA+ people may harbor prejudices against non-LGBTQIA+ people, thinking that they are fundamentally less tolerant or supportive. Those who are not LGBTQIA+ may harbor prejudices toward the LGBTQIA+ community based on false information, stereotypes, or personal convictions.

The collaboration will only be successful if these prejudices are overcome and trust and understanding are developed between the two populations.

Consequently, a society's political environment and cultural norms can provide serious obstacles to unification. LGBTQIA+ people may still experience severe shame, violence, persecution, and legal discrimination in some societies. In these situations, promoting LGBTQIA+ rights may be viewed as directly opposing cultural or religious norms, making it difficult to win over non-LGBTQIA+ people or groups.

Coming from firsthand experience, there are many issues that need to be settled within our community. I witnessed a lot of homophobia, biphobia, transphobia, aphobia (prejudice towards asexual and aromantic people), femme shaming, classism, sexism, casteism, racism, etc., displayed by our fellow community members. We must learn to accept that just because we may be drawn to a certain set of identities, it doesn't mean we should devalue or deny the existence of other identities if we want to achieve equity for everyone. Several cisgender homosexual or bisexual guys have asked me, "Why would I want to see feminine people on this dating app if I am attracted to men? " Here's the deal. In the case of gay or bisexual men, our attraction to boys and men does not necessitate that we perceive being a man as being masculine.

You must read the next chapter to see why I assert that being a man does not always entail being masculine. We have been misled into supporting a harmful social construct that tells us there is just one acceptable way to be a man. Yet, that is further from the truth. That also holds true for women and femininity. I firmly believe that what we ought to be celebrating is individuality. We should accept our own uniqueness while also extending that respect and appreciation to others. Every one of us has the right to live wholeheartedly. We have a right to happiness in who we are. We should be able to express ourselves through the things we wear, accessorize with, apply cosmetics to, behave in, etc. All of those things, after all, don't really indicate anything. Even a pink shirt is only a shirt. Even if they dangle, earrings are still just earrings. A dress with a high slit is still simply a dress. None of them are defined by gender. As genitalia themselves do not always indicate gender, we do not observe penises or vaginas on any of these items. I don't need to wear pants to identify as a man. A woman doesn't have to wear a dress to identify as a woman. We can wear whatever the hell we want and still identify as who we are.

Moving on, I believe it is ludicrous that we are such proud users of the term "gaydar" despite the fact that we preach against making assumptions about someone's identity based purely on their outward appearance. Such a word shouldn't even exist, in my personal view, and I myself avoid using it. In my opinion, people would be deterred from adopting particular looks they like out of concern that they would be assigned an incorrect identity. It could have an impact akin to deadnaming or misgendering. Moreover, it could trigger more severe queerphobia. Imagine presuming someone is queer and then approaching them based only on that false notion. Similar to how being effeminate is not an essential part of identifying as gay, being feminine is not a prerequisite for identifying as a transgender woman. Our community is extremely beautiful because of the number of possibilities available. What we need to practice is respectfully asking someone how they identify.

When asking someone about their identity, you need not know about the things you don't need to know. For instance, it is very inappropriate to inquire about what is between someone's legs. It isn't our concern. Relationship building shouldn't be dependent on one's genitalia. Matter of fact, any of the seven spectrums of attraction may be the origins of our attraction, yet they cannot serve as the standard for cultivating friendships. If we really want to advance the relationship, we ought to be sensitive when expressing our unique preferences. It's not very polite to directly inquire about someone's anatomy, though.

Let's discuss a highly complicated scenario that LGBTQIA+ people encounter—individuals who are secretly married. Have you ever used an LGBTQIA+ dating app just to discover that there is a shitload of married people there? Years ago, if you had asked me my opinion on this, I would have said that instead of cheating on their spouses, these people should have come out of the closet. Now, don't get me wrong. I still believe that cheating is absurd and wrong. However, It is really challenging to form an opinion on coming out instead of marrying someone you're not really attracted to. Coming out is also a personal decision that should only be made after carefully considering all factors. The individual alone must make this decision; no one else.

Let's use an example to better grasp this. In this example, we will consider an individual with the initials XYZ. Let us assume that XYZ was assigned male at birth, self-identifies as a man, uses he/him pronouns and is only attracted to men. He was brought up with extremely strict religious principles and is afraid that if he discloses his true identity, his family would disown him. He endures pressure from his family to get married as he gets older. He has no autonomy because of the pressure and terror that his religion, culture, and family instill inside of his psyche. He marries ABC—an individual who was assigned female at birth, self-identifies as a woman, uses she/her pronouns and is only attracted to men. Subsequently, under pressure from his family to have grandchildren, he "makes love" to his wife even though he loathes having sex with a woman (due to his attraction to men). Even after having one or two children with his wife, he is still dissatisfied. He yearns for intimacy with another man. He eventually reinstalls Grindr on his phone and starts dating other men without revealing that he is married. This continues for a while until eventually, ABC catches him in the act. They formally file for divorce and even choose joint custody of their young kids. His children eventually begin hating him for lying to them and breaking their mother's heart. Who do you believe is to blame for this? Is XYZ at fault for keeping his identity a secret? Is ABC at fault for not upholding the sanctity of the marriage? Are their children right to despise their father for being caught up in this stressful family drama? Do XYZ's parents deserve blame for forcing their son to live up to their standards? The answers to these queries are not straightforward. There are, in my opinion, several ways to look at this.

Let's look at this first from XYZ's point of view. In the first place, he didn't really have an option. He was taught to fear both God and society as a result of his upbringing in an orthodox household. He was forewarned that if he decided to accept his identity, his family and those close to him would subject him to psychological abuse. He would endure daily humiliation. Also, he could become the victim of a horrifying hate crime. There was a great deal to lose. His best option was to wed ABC in accordance with the toxic social norms. As I previously stated, he chose against coming out because he felt unsafe. This is why we have no right to criticize his choice. Secondly, he wasn't content with his life even though he had chosen to wed ABC. He didn't feel completely satisfied. He made the decision to lead a dual life since he yearned for intimacy with another man. That is undoubtedly an act of infidelity toward his wife, but he once more felt frustrated. He was compelled to do it covertly because he felt entrapped. It doesn't excuse the adultery, but it's still a decision he took since doing otherwise would have caused him emotional anguish. Finally, he kept his marriage a secret from the other men he met out of concern that they would reject him. What someone in this circumstance would be going through is beyond my ability to even conceive. Thus in my judgment, his decisions were reasonable given his circumstances, and he wouldn't be held responsible.

Should we thus hold ABC accountable for disrespecting her marriage to XYZ? Let's see the world through her eyes. Since ABC found men attractive, she married one without knowing his real identity. Given that she could have two children with him, she could have been content. She was able to provide her family the same, which was presumably what they expected of her as well. She thought she had checked all the boxes. But, finding her husband in bed with another man would undoubtedly have ripped her apart, similar to if XYZ had been discovered with another woman. She was entirely entitled to feel offended and upset. Before getting married, they had not discussed it in any conversations. If they had, they may have chosen to forgo marriage or keep their relationship open. The latter, though, might not have been favored by either of their families. She consequently filed for divorce after the discovery. I don't believe her choice to be incorrect. If she believed that XYZ's infidelity would follow her and disrupt her calm for the rest of her life, she made a sensible choice. After all, her happiness matters as well. She deserved to feel wanted by her spouse as well. Thus, no, I don't believe she should be made liable for her reaction.

So the children must be held accountable for harboring animosity toward their father, right? Let's investigate this. XYZ did indeed hurt ABC's feelings. Because he made conscious decisions, the act was additionally deliberate. He did, however, have a compelling reason. He weighed his options and decided it was too risky to come out. He felt safer emotionally and mentally leading a dual life. He assumed he could live his entire life following that course. But given that they have had greater exposure to a broader range of information, shouldn't his children accept him for who he is? Although it's possible that they do understand him as who he is, their main concern is undoubtedly the significant developments in their family. Due to their divorce, children would be sent back and forth between parents as minors. Divorce has a terrible impact on children's mental health as well. This is difficult for them to comprehend, and they could even take responsibility for their parent's divorce. Kids should be able to concentrate on their education, careers, and personal lives by living in a happy household. Therefore, I don't believe it is fair to hold the children accountable for being bitter with their father.

Hence, it is without a doubt that XYZ's parents are to blame for depriving him of a comfortable atmosphere and for imposing their expectations on him. But hold on! It is indeed likely that his parents were not adequately informed about the LGBTQIA+ community. That generation was presumably misinformed and misguided, which caused them to harbor prejudice toward our community.

Unlearning decades of rigid indoctrination that was practiced via education and religion is not simple for anyone. Not to mention the harsh colonial laws that carried the death penalty for anybody engaging in homosexual activity. They developed inflexible mindsets as a result of those same circumstances, which led them to think that adopting a more liberal view would be a grave sin.

If none of them are at fault, then who is? I suppose the structures created by the enforcers of colonialism and patriarchy are. They established a social order that required individuals to cede an excessive amount of power to the larger society. They were led to believe that adhering to toxic societal standards is the only way to receive respect from others. They were disabused of the notion that contentment is an outcome of possessing self-respect. These philosophies have survived until the modern day. We are always anxious about what other individuals will reckon if we don't meet their expectations. So what can XYZ's family members do? This would, in my opinion, depend on how well they are familiar with the LGBTQIA+ spectrum and understand that it is innate. All of them would need to discuss it openly and make an effort to comprehend XYZ's feelings and emotions. Each party involved would require varying amounts of time to fully process the information, thus this is something that would need to be discussed with compassion for one another. An effective alternative would be to seek the assistance of a mental health professional who is LGBTQIA+-affirming. These experts would be able to assist the family in reaching the optimal decision.

We as a community must also show compassion to those who are closeted. I've witnessed a lot of openly LGBTQIA+ people criticizing closeted peers for "not doing what is necessary". We must realize that coming out is not mandatory. Each person has the freedom to choose that for themselves. One's LGBTQIA+ identity is not invalidated by being closeted. They are as valid as any other LGBTQIA+ individual. In fact, we must do all in our power to help people who are having difficulties with their identities. We ought to empathize with them and do our best to help them along the way since, as members of the community who are out and proud, we have firsthand knowledge from having gone through the process.

I have heard many people use the phrase "That makes me feel uncomfortable" when they see LGBTQIA+ individuals living with authenticity and defying unrealistic cis-heteronormative standards. Most of them are cisgender men. This made me think, can someone else really make you uncomfortable when they don't even have control over your body? Hear me out on this one. Your entire body is solely under your control. You alone can move your eyes around and open or close them. You alone can move your legs and walk in all directions. You alone can move your heads around using your necks. The LGBTQIA+ community has not hacked into your brain and taken control of it. So how can we possibly make you feel uncomfortable when we simply exist in our own spaces? Your discomfort is your own making. You have a choice to either continue focusing on what you feel is uncomfortable to look at, or just use your body and look or walk away from it. It's so simple.

At the end of the day, we have a responsibility to respect not only ourselves but also other people for who they are. We are morally obligated to accept them as fellow humans, even if we don't understand their identities. Since change begins with each of us, it would be beneficial if we could be more open-minded and consider whether the information provided by the established systems is plausible. Progress can be hampered by the dissemination of false information from prejudiced groups to the public without first analyzing it for ourselves. It's a good idea to familiarize yourself with the LGBTQIA+ community, and I've made that process a bit simpler for you. So visit the next chapter to learn a bit more about our thriving community.

CHAPTER SIX

A GLIMPSE OF THE RAINBOW

Note: The definitions and terms included in this chapter are solely for educational purposes. I do not advocate assuming someone's assigned sex, gender identity or expression, sexual orientation, or romantic orientation based just on their outward appearance or mannerisms. I encourage you to always inquire about the preferred gender markers, sexual orientations, and pronouns of someone you meet. I also recommend that you speak to groups whose identities you are unfamiliar with using neutral terminology.

Introduction

Human beings can be grouped into several categories with respect to their identity — based on their biology, appearance, behavioral characteristics, psychology, faith or beliefs, sexual attraction, political affiliation, nationality, ethnicity, etc. Well because we're discussing the LGBTQIA+ community (or the "Alphabet/Rainbow Community," as some might prefer to call it), it's crucial to comprehend the concepts that follow. Knowing the distinction between these terms is essential as misinformation often results in misunderstanding or even prejudice:

- **Biological Sex:** At the time of birth, an individual receives a biological identifier called their "sex." It is determined by the external genitalia, chromosome combination, anatomy of the internal reproductive system, and gonad type. While certain ambiguities may be present from birth, others may not be apparent until later in life as a result of anatomical and hormonal changes. Hence, the range of biological sex is expansive. Eg.: Male.
- **Gender:** Rather than being biologically determined, gender is an identity based on the established social and cultural distinction of the sexes and the behaviors expected of each. It is frequently said by social conceptions that it falls within the binary. Despite the societal acceptance of alternative genders in various societies, people are frequently required to fit into one of the two gender roles that correspond to their apparent sex at birth. Eg. Female/Girl/Woman/Feminine.
- **Gender Identity:** It is an identifier that a person gives to themselves as they come to terms with who they truly are. The alignment of this self-identification with their biological sex or socially constructed gender roles is entirely dependent on psychological factors. Gender identity is a spectrum because everyone is wired differently. Eg.: Non-binary.
- **Gender Expression:** Frequently referred to as mannerism, it is a term used to identify a person's preferred means of self-expression. It may (or it may

not) match their gender or gender identity. It is also intrinsic and has the ability to locate itself anywhere throughout its spectrum. Eg.: Feminine.

- **Sexual Orientation:** This is a label, or combination of labels, that a person gives to themselves as they come to terms with their sexual or emotional attraction towards another person. Akin to gender, sexuality is intrinsic and may span a wide range of expressions. Eg.: Heterosexual.
- **Romantic Orientation:** This is a label, or cluster of labels, that a person gives to themselves when they come to terms with their romantic attraction towards another person. Comparable to gender and sexual orientation, there are several spectrums of romantic orientation. Eg.: Panromantic.

Terminology

Let's now take a look at the spectrum of terminology, including but not limited to those in the acronym LGBTQIA+. This list does not include all the terms that exist but are some of the rather basic, more common ones. Because the language associated with the community is constantly evolving, it is impossible to compile a list of every term.

- **LGBTQIA+:** The words lesbian, gay, bisexual, transgender, queer/questioning, intersex, and asexual/ aromantic are all referred to by this acronym. The plus sign (+) denotes the abundance of non-straight and non-cisgender identities, while the letter "A" does not stand for allies.

- **Female:** It is the sex that is physiologically endowed with a female reproductive system and mammary glands that produce milk in their breasts to nourish their young. They create ova, a type of female gamete that, when fertilized by a sperm, develops into an embryo. Females have two copies of the X chromosome, one of which is used to generate the egg or ovary, whereas men have an X and Y sex chromosome. The X or Y chromosome found in the male gamete aids in determining the sex of the fetus.

- **Male:** It is the physiological sex, which has a male reproductive system composed of testosterone produced as a result of the Y-chromosome being a part of their genetic makeup. Men possess both the X and Y chromosomes. They contribute either an X or Y chromosome, which is transmitted during sexual reproduction by a male gamete called a sperm. Although males have mammary glands as well, they are unable to make milk because of low levels of the hormone prolactin, which is responsible for the process. With the use of medicine, prolactin levels can be raised, which in turn stimulates lactation.

- **Intersex:** It is a term used to describe people who are born with different sex characteristics, such as chromosomes, gonads, sex hormones, and/or genitalia, which do not correspond to the traditional binary notions of male or female bodies. While some intersex characteristics are apparent at birth, others don't become visible until much later in life, usually until puberty.

- **Dyadic:** It pertains to individuals who are not considered intersex. Since no one genuinely falls into the dyadic (two-part) system of determining sex, some intersex persons prefer that those who aren't intersex refer to themselves as "non-intersex".

- **Biological Sex Spectrum:** Our biology is indeed not binary; rather, it exists on a spectrum, and this is the notion and reality behind it. Human sex cannot be purely male or female because we also have alternative chromosomal combinations (such as X, XXX, XXY, XYY, etc.) in conjunction to the XX and XY sex chromosomes.
- **Sex Assignment:** It is the determination of a newborn's sex at birth. The common procedure for doing this is to examine the infant's genitalia. Any ambiguities may affect the newborn's sex assignment, owing to an inconsistent phenotypical sex assignment. If these ambiguities are not present at birth, they may develop later in life as a result of changes in the hormonal balance and/or reproductive anatomy of the individual. If there are any obvious uncertainties at birth, they are frequently "corrected" medically to fit one of the two sexes.
- **Assigned Male At Birth (AMAB):** It is also known as Male Assigned At Birth (MAAB) and Designated Male At Birth (DMAB), and it is used to identify a person of any age, regardless of their gender identity, whose sex assignment at birth resulted in a declaration of "male."
- **Assigned Female At Birth (AFAB):** It is also known as Female Assigned At Birth (FAAB) and Designated Female At Birth (DFAB), and it is used to identify a person of any age, regardless of their gender identity, whose sex assignment at birth resulted in a declaration of "female."
- **Unassigned At Birth (UAAB):** It is employed by parents who want to raise gender-neutral kids. Because of this,

the individual is free to identify as whichever gender best suits their physical characteristics and psychological makeup.

- **Sex Reassignment:** It is a healthcare approach that combines psychological, medical, and surgical techniques in order to physically modify an individual's sex characteristics. This process is commonly known as Gender-affirming Care. This is typically chosen by transgender people who believe that there is a discrepancy between their assigned sex and their physical attributes and who want to align their sex characteristics with their gender identity. It is also used to medically correct visibly ambiguous genitalia in intersex babies, despite fierce opposition from human rights groups.
- **Body Image:** It is a term used to describe how one feels, behaves, and appears to think about their body and is typically influenced by communities, families, media, cultures, and our own perspectives.
- **Body Policing:** It is any activity that seeks to (intentionally or inadvertently; directly or indirectly) influence or modify another people's actions regarding their own physical body, typically with reference to size or gender expression.
- **Gender Binary:** Under this system, people are expected to fit into one of two categories of gender roles, gender identities, and characteristics based on their genitalia: male/boy/man/masculine and female/girl/woman/ feminine. For intersex people, invasive surgical sex reassignment is used to drive them to conform to the binary.
- **Man:** It is a gender identity that adult male humans adopt to identify themselves. They are known as boys

until they reach maturity.

- **Woman:** It is a gender identity that adult female humans adopt to identify themselves. They are known as girls until they reach maturity.
- **Womxn:** In an effort to move away from the term "men" in the traditional spelling of women, some women spell the word with an "x" as a symbol of their empowerment.
- **Gender Role:** It is also known as the "sex role," and it refers to the boundaries of attitudes and behaviors that are deemed acceptable, appropriate, or desirable based on one's biological or perceived sex.
- **Cisgender:** It is a term used to describe someone whose gender identity matches the sex assigned to them at birth and is frequently abbreviated to just "cis."
- **Genderism:** It is a pervasive system of exclusion and discrimination that goes by the name of cissexism and is based on the idea that there are only two genders. It also supports the notion that a person's assigned sex and gender and associated characteristics are interrelated. As a result, it discriminates against people whose gender identity or gender expression deviates from socially acceptable norms. In this ideology, cisgender people are seen as being superior to and dominating over transgender and gender-nonconforming people.
- **Cissexism:** It is an ideology that prioritizes and cherishes cisgender identities and persons to the detriment of trans people. It permeates all aspects of society.
- **Heteronormativity:** It is the presumption that everyone is heterosexual and that heterosexuality is superior to all other sexual orientations, and is held by people or institutions.

- **Heterosexism:** It is the belief that everyone should or is heterosexual. While offering advantages to heterosexual persons, heterosexism marginalizes the needs, concerns, and life experiences of LGBTQIA+ people. It is a form of oppression that serves to strengthen the institutional, societal, and cultural realities of erasure and silencing.
- **Monosexism:** It is the idea that monosexuality is more favorable than other sexual orientations, such as bisexuality, omnisexuality, polyamory, and pansexuality. Some individuals believe bisexuals to be promiscuous.
- **Acephobia:** It is the aversion, hostility, or prejudice toward asexual individuals.
- **Arophobia:** It is the rejection of aromantic individuals out of fear, hatred, or bigotry.
- **Homophobia:** It is the hostility, dread, and/or condemnation of those who are attracted to other people of the same gender. Prejudice, discrimination, harassment, and violent acts motivated by fear and hatred are all examples of homophobia. It is prevalent on a social, institutional, and individual level and is strongly related to transphobia, biphobia, and other phobias.
- **Biphobia:** It is the aversion, hostility, or prejudice toward those who are attracted to persons of different genders.
- **Transphobia:** It is an expression of fear, hostility, and discrimination towards persons whose perceived gender or gender identities do not match social expectations of their ascribed sex or gender. This is institutionally, culturally, and individually enforced.

- **Transmisogyny:** It is prejudice towards transgender individuals and transfeminine people; the especially violent intersection that fosters misogyny and transphobia.
- **Gender Dysphoria:** It is the psychological anguish that someone experiences as a result of a mismatch between their gender identity and the sex they were assigned at birth. An individual may have self-esteem issues, suicidal thoughts, sadness, anxiety, and social isolation as a result. Support for the same condition can be obtained through changes in gender expression, counseling, and transitioning with the use of hormone therapy or surgery. Transgender individuals are more likely to experience gender dysphoria.
- **Transgender:** Trans is a general term that is frequently used to refer to people who identify as someone other than the sex that was assigned to them at birth. Also, it covers persons who are neither exclusively male nor female (those who are non-binary or genderqueer, including crossdressers, bigender, pangender, genderfluid, or agender).
- **Transitioning:** It is a process wherein a person alters their sex characteristics and/or gender expression to better align with their internal sense of gender identity. Those who identify as transgender often undergo this, whether medically through hormone replacement treatment or surgically through sex reassignment.
- **Transsexual:** This term describes transgender individuals who undergo a long-term transition to the sex or gender with which they identify. They usually choose hormone replacement therapy or sex reassignment surgery to help their bodies conform to their identified sex or gender.

- **Cross Dresser:** It is a term used to describe people who dress, at least partially, as a gender other than their assigned sex and was formerly known as transvestite.
- **Drag King:** This term is used to describe people who present themselves as men, usually during an act or performance. It doesn't always correspond to a person's gender identity.
- **Drag Queen:** This term is used to describe people who present themselves as women, usually during an act or performance. It doesn't always correspond to a person's gender identity.
- **Gender Variance:** It also goes by the name gender nonconformity and describes a person's behavior or gender expression that deviates from traditional gender roles for men and women. People who display gender variance may be described as transgender or gender variant in their gender identity, as well as gender-variant, gender-non-conforming, gender-diverse, or non-binary. Gender variance may also be evident in some intersex people.
- **Gender Expansive:** Those who widen their own culture's conceptions of gender identities, expression, roles, and other gender conventions use this general word. It includes people who identify as transgender or anyone else who appears to be expanding the traditional ideas of gender in society.
- **Gender Outlaw:** People who reject traditional male and female ideologies use this term to describe themselves.
- **Non-binary:** It is a spectrum of gender identities that fall outside of the gender binary and is also referred to as genderqueer. Since many non-binary people identify with a gender other than their assigned sex, this could fall under the trans category.

- **Bigender:** It is used to identify people who exhibit any two gender identities and behaviors and is also known as dual gender. Having two distinct gender identities or alternating between them, one may identify as both a man and a woman or move between masculine and feminine gender expressions.
- **Agender:** It is a term used by those who identify as having no gender or not having a gender identity. It is also known as genderless, genderfree, non-gendered, or ungendered. Those who identify as any of these may not necessarily self-identify as transgender, despite the fact that it embraces a variety of identities that do not follow conventional gender standards.
- **Demigender:** It is the gender identity of a person who, despite the sex assigned to them at birth, identifies primarily or partially with one gender, even when other aspects of their identity may be allocated to several genders.
- **Genderfluid:** This is a phrase used by those who prefer to adhere to several definitions of gender identity rather than conform to a single one. They might switch between gender expressions or simultaneously display several features of various gender markers. They might also describe themselves as bi-gender, which involves seesawing between masculine and feminine, or as trigender, which involves vacillating between these and a third gender.
- **Neutrois:** It falls under the transgender or genderqueer categories and is a non-binary gender identity. There is no specific definition for this term as each of those who identify as such experience their gender differently. The most typical ones are agender, genderless, neither male nor female, neutral-gender, and null-gender.

- **Fa'afafine:** These people are regarded as belonging to the third gender in Samoan society. Despite being anatomically male, they dress and act in ways that are more typically feminine. They are not denigrated or subjected to discrimination since they are acknowledged as a natural gender. They are only drawn to heterosexual, macho guys.
- **Hijra:** In certain Asian societies, they are people who are regarded as neither men nor women. While some of them have a feminine physical makeup, the majority are either male or intersex. They play the third gender role, but in their societies, they are not treated with the same respect and acceptance as men and women.
- **Khanith:** In Oman, these people make up a third gender that is recognized. These are male gay prostitutes who dress in feminine mannerisms and pastel colors rather than white, which is the hue worn by other men. Men can interact with females, and they frequently do so during weddings and other formal occasions. They run their own homes and take care of all the duties (both male and female). They are nevertheless able to marry women and, by doing so, demonstrate their manhood in the same way as males in their community may by doing so. These men can restore their position as khaniths at the subsequent wedding should a divorce or death occur.
- **Two-spirit:** This term, which is also known as "two-spirited," refers to indigenous North American people who identify with gender identities other than that of cisgender men and women. Certain sections of the community view it as a category rather than an identity, choosing to identify with gender terms that are peculiar to their culture or nation.

- **Misgendering:** It is the concept of assigning a person's gender that isn't congruent with their gender identity. This could happen as a result of the use of pronouns, the use of terminology that is exclusive to one gender, or the classification of people into one gender or the other based solely on the way they appear.
- **Deadnaming:** It refers to employing a name that a transgender or non-binary person used prior to transitioning, such as their birth name.
- **Omnigender:** Literally, it means possessing all genders. It is employed in opposition to the notion that there are only two genders.
- **Pangender:** Those that display characteristics of multiple genders use this term, also known as polygender, to purposefully challenge the idea that there are only two genders.
- **Pronouns:** These are linguistic devices for third-person referencing people. Certain languages and cultural traditions connect these to the gender binary, which frequently leads to misgendering.
- **Questioning:** Identifying one's gender identity, gender expression, and/or sexual orientation is the first step in this process. Those who identify as LGBTQIA+ may use this term to describe themselves.
- **Masculine:** It is a term used to define a collection of attributes, behaviors, and roles that are believed to be appropriate, fitting, and expected of boys and men. Masculinity may be displayed by people of various gender identities as their gender expression, therefore it is not solely a characteristic of the male human.
- **Feminine:** It is a term used to define a collection of attributes, behaviors, and roles that are believed to be appropriate, fitting, and expected of girls and women.

Femininity may be displayed by people of various gender identities as their gender expression, therefore it is not solely a characteristic of the female human.

- **Effeminate:** It is a term used to describe boys or men who manifest traits that are often associated with feminine nature.
- **Tomboyish:** It is a term used to describe girls or women who manifest traits that are often associated with masculine nature.
- **Butch:** It is a term used to describe a masculine gender expression in lesbian and queer women.
- **Femme:** It is a term used to describe a feminine gender expression in lesbian and queer women.
- **Androgyny:** It is a term used to describe a combination of masculine and feminine characteristics in an ambiguous form. It may be used to define a biological sex, gender identity, gender expression, or sexual identity. Intersex persons are frequently mentioned when biological sex is being discussed. It refers to people who identify as non-binary, genderqueer, or gender-neutral as their gender identity. It can be achieved as a gender expression through personal grooming, fashion, or hormone therapy.
- **Allosexual:** Also known as zedsexual, it refers to people who are not on the asexual spectrum. In other words, it refers to a person who frequently feels attracted sexually to others. However, it is not always a reference to a sexual identity in isolation. It is a catch-all term coined by the a-spec community to describe anyone who is not asexual.
- **Asexual Spectrum:** It is a spectrum of sexual orientations that are collectively referred to as asexual. People who fall on the asexual spectrum may not feel

any sexual attraction at all or may only feel a small amount of it, making them more sympathetic to the asexual experience than the allosexual experience. People on the asexual spectrum are connected by the fact that they do not experience sexual attraction at the "normal" degree or in the "standard" manner.

- **Heterosexual:** Often referred to as straight, it is used to identify individuals who are sexually attracted to the members of the opposite sex. It may be contested that the definition might employ "other genders" instead of opposing gender, because gender identity rests on a non-exhaustive spectrum not contained within the binary. This can also suggest that heterosexuality and pansexuality may overlap.
- **Homosexual:** Also knows as gay, it is a term used to describe individuals who are sexually attracted to the same gender. Although the term gay is widely used by men, and lesbian by women, homosexual is mostly used in clinical contexts.
- **Gay:** Although it can be used to generally describe an individual who is sexually attracted to the same gender, it is most widely used by men who are sexually attracted to other men.
- **Lesbian:** It is a term used to describe women who are sexually attracted to other women.
- **Bisexual:** Though widely assumed to be a term for identifying individuals sexually attracted to men and women, it is a term used to describe an individual who is attracted to to or more gender identities.
- **Pansexual:** It is a term used to identify individuals who are sexually attracted to people regardless of their biological sex or gender identity.

- **Demisexual:** It is used to describe individuals under the graysexual umbrella who experience a sexual attraction only towards persons with whom they have an emotional bond.
- **Graysexual:** It is a term used to describe a persons who may only experience sexual attraction on occasion. Gray-sexuality is thought to be the range between asexuality and allosexuality.
- **Aceflux:** It is a sexual orientation on the asexual spectrum. It is defined as someone whose sexual orientation fluctuates but generally stays on the asexual spectrum. An aceflux individual may feel aggressively asexual one day and less asexual another day, and may also feel demisexual or grey asexual at times. Some aceflux people may feel like they are allosexual at times.
- **Aromantic Spectrum:** It is a collection of romantic orientations that collectively are referred to as aromantic. Aromantic people may not feel any romantic attraction to anybody, may feel it is lacking, or may feel romantic attraction to one gender over another.
- **Aromantic:** It is used to identify an individual who does not experience any romantic attraction towards anyone.
- **Heteroromantic:** It is used to identify individuals who experience a romantic attraction towards persons of the opposite gender.
- **Homoromantic:** It is used to identify individuals who experience a romantic attraction towards persons of the same gender.
- **Biromantic:** It is used to identify individuals who experience a romantic attraction towards two or more genders, or persons of the same and other genders. Sometimes used the same way as panromantic.

- **Panromantic:** It is used to identify individuals who experience a romantic attraction towards persons of any, every, and all genders.
- **Demiromantic:** It is used to distinguish people who are attracted romantically to others but do so only after developing a strong emotional connection with them.
- **Greyromantic:** It is used to identify people who only occasionally or in specific situations feel attracted to someone romantically.
- **Aroflux:** It is a romantic orientation on the aromantic spectrum, defined as someone whose romantic orientation fluctuates but generally stays on the aromantic spectrum. An aroflux person may feel very strongly aromantic one day and less aromantic another day, they might feel demiromantic or greyromantic at times. Some aroflux individuals may occasionally feel alloromantic.
- **Queer:** It is a derogatory phrase that some individuals chose to reclaim for themselves and use in a variety of contexts. For example, it can be used as a personal identity to indicate that one is not both straight and cisgender without necessarily disclosing anything else or as an umbrella term for LGBTQIA+ identities. Although its usage is common, it is inadvisable since it harms those who do not wish to have this slur applied to them; it also indicates defiance of heteronormativity and cisnormativity.
- **Coming Out:** It is the act of revealing one's LGBTQIA+ identity to others. People are presumed to be straight, cisgender, and dyadic/non-intersex irrespective of whether demonstrated otherwise, hence coming out is a continuous process. Someone could be out about specific identities or out to specific individuals, but not

to others.

- **Closeted:** It describes a member of the LGBTQIA+ community who has chosen to keep their identity concealed from others. In a heterosexist and cissexist culture, it can often be crucial to be in the closet for an individual's protection from persecution. The decision of how, when, and whether to come out is an individual choice that should be respected. A person may be openly gay or bisexual in some situations yet closed off in others.
- **Outing:** It is the unintentional exposure of another person's intersex, transgender identity, or any marginalized sexual or romantic orientation.
- **Internalized Oppression:** It is the dread and loathing of one's own oppressed identity. Many LGBTQIA+ persons have consciously or unconsciously learned that they are less important than straight, cisgender people due to institutional heterosexism and cissexism.
- **Ally:** This term describes someone who relentlessly challenges heterosexism, biphobia, homophobia, transphobia, transmisogyny, acephobia, heterosexual privilege, etc. in oneself and others. Action is necessary to be an ally; goodwill alone is insufficient. Members of the affected minority group alone can assess the nature and legitimacy of one's allyship.

Conclusion

These are just a few of the terms and definitions that the LGBTQIA+ community seems to use or has historically used. In addition to these, there are countless others constantly emerging. So, it is always a good idea to stay informed about at least the fundamental, simple ones. The best course of action is to appreciate everyone utilizing them and treat them as you would yourself, even if you don't understand any of them.

The LGBTQIA+ community encompasses a wide range of identities, all of which are wholly legitimate. Taking into account the multiple intersections with so many different groups, we are arguably the most inclusive community in the entire world. With the frequent stereotyping by privileged persons, it may appear difficult to accept that the world is so diverse, but it is crucial that we utilize our ability to reason to recognize that we are all inherently distinct.

References

- Middle Assyrian Law Code
- Avesta, Vendidad, Fargard 8. Funerals and purification, unlawful sex
- A Timeline of Gay World History
- Oremus Bible Browser
- Encyclopedia of Homosexuality Vol. 2 by Wayne R. Dynes
- Homophobia: A History by Byrne R. S.Fone
- Historical Dictionary of the Lesbian and Gay Liberation Movements by JoAnne Myers
- A History of Homophobia: 3 The Later Roman Empire & The Early Middle Ages by Rictor Norton
- Internet History Sourcebooks, History Department of Fordham University, New York
- Corpus Iuris Civilis: The Digest and Codex: Marriage Laws
- The Visigothic Code: (Forum judicum) by S. P. Scott, The Library of Iberian Resources
- Europe and homosexuality, SGS
- Burned for Sodomy, Queer Saints and Martyrs
- Homosexuality and Civilization, Louis Crompton, Cambridge & London: Belknap Press of Harvard University Press, 2003
- Nezahualcoyotl's Law Code (1431)
- The History of Sodomy Laws in the United States by George Painter
- Looking back at Quebec queer life since the 17th century by Richard Burnett

- Demmark, Pioneer In The Rights For The LGBT by Ana García Gutiérrez
- The Raid on Mother Clap's Molly House by Rictor Norton
- Passions of the Cut Sleeve: The Male Homosexual Tradition in China by Bret Hinsch
- The A to Z of Homosexuality by Brent L. Pickett
- Famous GLBT & GLBTI People, Dr. Magnus Hirschfeld by Raymond Melville
- Warsaw by John D. Stanley
- Prejudice And Pride: Discrimination Against Gay People In Modern Britain by Bruce Galloway
- Netherlands Scientific Humanitarian Committee, Wikipedia
- Encyclopedia of Lesbian and Gay Histories and Cultures, edited by George Haggerty, Bonnie Zimmerman
- Before Stonewall: Activists For Gay And Lesbian Rights In Historical Context by Vern L. Bullough
- Stonewall then and now: Harvard scholars reflect on the history and legacy of the milestone gay-rights demonstrations triggered by a police raid at a dive bar in Manhattan, The Harvard Gazette
- Alan Turing: a short biography by Andrew Hodges
- The Wildeblood scandal: the trial that rocked 1950s Britain – and changed gay rights by Adam Mars-Jones, The Guardian
- Man imprisoned for being gay to get posthumous pardon from Trudeau, CBC News
- Governor Vetoes Gay Job Bias Bill : Discrimination: Wilson says legislation is bad for business. Its author calls action 'cave-in to the right.', Los Angeles Times

- Gay Rights, Military Wrongs: Political Perspectives on Lesbians and Gays in The Military, edited by Craig A. Rimmerman
- Stonewall riots, Wikipedia
- LGBT rights in Nicaragua, Wikipedia
- Transgender Day of Remembrance, Wikipedia
- Matthew Shepard, Wikipedia
- Timeline of LGBT history, Wikipedia
- LGBT rights in the 19th century, Wikipedia
- Timeline of LGBT history, 20th century, Wikipedia
- Earliest Italy: An Overview of the Italian Paleolithic and Mesolithic by Margherita Mussi
- Grave of stone age transsexual excavated in Prague, Archeology News Network
- Gay Awareness: Discovering the Heart of the Father and the Mind of Christ on Sexuality by Landon Schott
- The Construction of Homosexuality by David F. Greenberg
- Same-Sex Unions in Pre-Modern Europe by John Boswell
- The History by Herodotus
- Symposium by Plato
- Current Concepts in Transgender Identity by Dallas Denny
- Timeline of LGBT history, 21st century, Wikipedia
- Timeline of asexual history, Wikipedia
- LGBT history in India, Wikipedia

Share Your Honest Opinions About This Book

Please share your opinions regarding this book with me. Working on it has been an enjoyable experience.

On the product page of the retailer (Notion Press, Amazon, Flipkart, etc.) where you purchased your copy of this book, you can leave your review along with your criticism. It would also mean a lot to me if you recommend this book to someone else.

About The Author

Francis H. Fernandes, also known as "The Emo Poet," was born and raised in The State of Kuwait, a tiny Middle Eastern peninsula nation. In 2016, he began writing, primarily with poetry and short quotes. His writing is inspired by the challenges he has endured in life and also incorporates the sufferings of other individuals. He started reading books and penning his own songs not too long ago. He adopted "The Emo Poet" as his pen name on his social media in September 2019. (Facebook and Instagram).

Francis is a co-founder and former Chairman of the Goa Rainbow Trust, an NGO based in Goa, India for the welfare of the LGBTQIA+ community. He is an openly gay, androgynous (in terms of how he expresses his gender), homoromantic demisexual (an identity that lies on the asexuality spectrum), and demisexual writer. " I'm Human Too", one of his first poems on diversity, encourages people to treat one another with respect and recognize each other as fellow human beings. In his own words, "diversity is acceptable, divisiveness is not." He is certain that the world may be improved for coming generations through love and acceptance of diversity.